Skills in English

English

Level 1

Listening

Teacher's Book

Terry Phillips

and

Anna Phillips

Garnet
EDUCATION

Published by
Garnet Publishing Ltd.
8 Southern Court
South Street
Reading RG1 4QS, UK

ISBN 1 85964 774 X

British Library Cataloguing-in-Publication Data
A catalogue record for this book is available from
the British Library.

Production
Project manager: Richard Peacock
Editorial team: Nicky Platt, Lucy Thompson, John Bates,
                   Katharine Mendelsohn
Art director: David Rose
Design: Mark Slader
Typesetting: Samantha Barden
Illustration: Beehive Illustration (Roger Wade Walker),
                   Doug Nash, Karen Rose, Ian West
Photography: Corbis (Chris Lisle), Digital Vision,
                   Flat Earth, Image Source, Photodisc

Garnet Publishing wishes to thank the following for their
assistance in the development of this project:
Dr Abdullah Al Khanbashi, Abderrazak Ben Hamida,
Maxine Gillway, Glenys Roberts and the Level 1 team at
UGRU, UAE University

Every effort has been made to trace the copyright holders
and we apologize in advance for any unintentional
omissions. We will be happy to insert the appropriate
acknowledgements in any subsequent editions.

Audio production: John Green TEFL Tapes

Printed and bound
in Lebanon by International Press

Skills in English
Listening   Level 1

Contents

Book Map

Theme	Listening text type	Hearing consonants	Hearing vowels	Aural skills
1 Education, Student Life	Speech	/p/, /b/	Short vs long: /ɪ/ vs /iː/	• Understanding spoken definitions • Following instructions • Identifying names
2 Daily Life, Schedules	Lecture		Short vs long: /æ/ vs /ɑː/	• Understanding spoken times
3 Work and Business, Work Starts Now!	Lecture	/g/, /dʒ/		• Identifying important words • Predicting content
4 Science and Nature, So You Want to Be a Scientist?	Radio programme	/θ/, /ð/	Short vs long: /e/ vs /ɜː/	• Predicting the next word
5 The Physical World, Where Is Your Country?	Lecture	/s/, /z/	Short vs long: /ɒ/ vs /ɔː/	• Understanding spoken spellings
6 Culture and Civilization, Congratulations!	Student talk	/t/, /d/	Long: /uː/	• Understanding signpost language (1)
7 They Made Our World, Who? What? When?	Lecture	/ʃ/, /tʃ/		• Understanding signpost language (2) • Identifying dates
8 Art and Literature, There Was Once a Poor Man ...	Radio programme		Diphthongs: /aɪ/, /eɪ/, /ɔɪ/	• Following a narrative
9 Sports and Leisure, Classifying Sports	Lecture		Diphthongs: /əʊ/, /aʊ/	• Recognising important words
10 Nutrition and Health, Nutrients and Food Groups	Lecture	Revision	Revision	• Revision

INTRODUCTION

The series

This course is part of the four-level *Skills in English* series. The series as a whole prepares students to study wholly or partly in English medium at tertiary level.

In addition, there is a remedial / false beginner course, *Starting Skills in English*, for students who are not ready to begin Level 1.

At each level there are four courses, each dealing with a discrete skill: Listening, Speaking, Reading or Writing. The focus in a particular course is very definitely on that skill. The methodology notes below repeatedly stress the discrete skills focus, and caution against spending too much time on, for example, Speaking, in this Listening Skills course. This is not because the writer dislikes integrated skills. The insistence on the target skill is because the writer believes that some students need one or two skills more than the others, and that students should be allowed to make differential progress in the four skills rather than constantly being held to the level at which they can hear, say, read and write a common set of language items.

In all four skills books, the course is organised into 10 themes, each with particular thematic focus. The 10 themes are:

Theme 1: Education
Theme 2: Daily Life
Theme 3: Work and Business
Theme 4: Science and Nature
Theme 5: The Physical World
Theme 6: Culture and Civilization
Theme 7: They Made Our World
Theme 8: Art and Literature
Theme 9: Sports and Leisure
Theme 10: Nutrition and Health

If you are using other skills books in the series, we recommend that you use them in the following sequence:

Listening
Speaking
Reading
Writing

The commonality of theme across the four skills means that the more skills books you use, the deeper and wider the students' linguistic ability to communicate in that thematic area becomes.

This course

This is the Listening Skills course at Level 1. The aim is to introduce students with an elementary level of general English to the basic skills involved in understanding lectures in English.

The course comprises the Student's Book, this Teacher's Book, three CDs or cassettes containing all the listening material, and a Test Booklet.

The course stands alone – in other words, it is not necessary for students to have studied any of the other skills courses in order to benefit from this course.

The Test Booklet contains one test for each theme, a revision test after Themes 1 to 5 and a final test. The tests are sold in packs of ten, with an answer and marking guide. In addition, when you purchase a pack of ten booklets, you get access to an alternative final test on the skillsinenglish.com website. Methodology notes on administering the tests are provided in the answer and marking guide.

Organisation of the course

Each theme contains four lessons. Each lesson has a clear focus and purpose, as follows:

Lesson	Focus	Purpose and methodology points
1	Vocabulary	To ensure that students understand and can recognise basic vocabulary that will be needed for the theme.
2	Listening	To practise the listening skill; this lesson revises the aural skills and the segmental features taught in previous themes.
3	Learning new skills	To highlight specific listening skills of two types: **a** segmental features such as individual phonemes and minimal pairs; **b** broad aural skills such as *understanding signpost language.*

| 4 | Applying new skills | To apply skills learnt in Lesson 3 to a new text – usually a parallel text to that in Lesson 2. |

Vocabulary

As can be seen from the information about the organisation of the course above, the writer is firmly committed to the importance of vocabulary. This is why one lesson out of every four is devoted to vocabulary and why, in addition, the first activity in many of the other three lessons in each theme is a vocabulary revision exercise. In the case of listening, students must be able to recognise a wide range of words in isolation and, even more importantly, in the stream of speech.

In Lesson 1, key vocabulary is printed down the outer margin. The positioning is deliberate. You and the students should be able to flick back and find a thematic set easily.

There are two sets of words in each case:

The red words

These are all from the Council of Europe Waystage level, organised into thematic sets. It is assumed that students correctly placed at this level will know all or most of these from previous language learning. If they do not, you will need to supplement the one or two exercises provided. Students are required to manipulate the words in a number of ways, largely to prove that they understand the meaning. Thus, activities require them to discuss questions using the red words, put the red words into lexical sets or make true sentences about themselves, their family, country, etc., using the red words.

The green words

These are high-frequency words from the thematic set that will be required for the listening texts in Lessons 2 or 4. It is essential that, by the end of this lesson, the students understand the meaning of these words *and* can correctly pick them out from the stream of speech, so that they do not cause problems with comprehension in the later lessons.

In Lessons 2, 3 and 4, there are additional words that will almost certainly be new to the students. Some of these require pre-teaching, in which case there are additional vocabulary activities at the start of the relevant lesson. In most cases, however, these new words are defined in the listening texts themselves or deducible from context. Clearly, the ability to wait for definitions in a text and to work out meaning from spoken context are key listening skills; therefore, these new items should not be pre-taught. However, once the students have had the opportunity to understand the items in context, it is quite reasonable to focus on the new vocabulary and try to ensure that some, at least, is remembered in the future.

To enable you and the students to keep track of the thematic sets, these are reproduced at the back of this book and the Student's Book. In addition, they are organised alphabetically with their origins (i.e., as a red or green word) retained.

Grammar

According to recent corpora research, the main tense that appears in academic text is the simple present. This tense alone accounts for the vast majority of sentences. At the other extreme, in one corpus of four million words, there was only one example of the present perfect continuous. This suggests that we should not spend a huge amount of time on verb tenses in an EAP course. Instead, we need to ensure that students can understand and produce compound and complex sentences in the simple present tense. Rather than in verb tenses, difficulty in academic texts often lies in the use of complex noun phrases with a great deal of pre- and post-modification of the head word, and in the use of long subordinate clauses at the start of sentences. For this reason, *Skills in English* first ensures that students can understand and produce basic SVO patterns and then, gradually, can understand and produce expansion of the S and O and combinations of SVO sentences in various ways.

Skills Checks

These are a key feature of the course. In every theme, there is at least one Skills Check box. The naming of this feature is significant. It is assumed that the students will have heard about most, if not all, of the skills points in these boxes – i.e., they are skills *checks*, not skills *presentations*. It is the writer's experience that many students who have gone through a modern language course have *heard of the* majority of skills points but cannot make practical use of them. If you feel in a particular case that the students have no idea about the point in question, spend considerably longer on a full presentation.

In most cases, the students are given an activity to do before looking at the Skills Check box. Thus, a test-teach-test approach is used. This is quite deliberate. With this approach, there is a good chance that the students will be sensitised to the particular point before being asked to understand it intellectually. This is likely to be more effective than talking about the point and then asking the students to try to apply it.

Specific activities

Certain types of activity are repeated on several occasions throughout the book. This is because these activities are particularly valuable in language learning.

Crosswords and puzzles

One of the keys to vocabulary learning is repetition. However, the repetition must be active. It is no good if students are simply going through the motions. The course uses crosswords and other kinds of puzzles to bring words back into consciousness through an engaging activity.

Odd one out

The ability to see the connections between linguistic items – and, therefore, the odd one out – is a key indicator of comprehension. However, it is often easier to see the odd one out than it is to explain why that item is different. This is why reasons are sometimes given. Where they are not, consider writing the reasons on the board, in jumbled order, if you feel your students will struggle without them.

Gap fill

Filling in missing words or phrases in a sentence or a text, or labelling a map or diagram, indicates comprehension of both the missing items and the context in which they correctly fit. It is generally better to provide the missing items to ensure that all the required items are available to all the students. In the case of Lesson 1, the words are usually available in the word list on the right. In other cases, you might prefer to supply the words or phrases on the board.

In addition, you can vary the approach to gap fills by sometimes going through the activity with the whole class, orally, pens down, then setting the same task individually. Gap fills or labelling activities can be photocopied and set as revision at the end of the unit or later, with or without the missing items box.

Two-column activities

This type of activity is generally better than open-ended questions or gap fill with no box of missing items, as it ensures that all the target language is available to the students. However, the activity is only fully effective if the two columns are dealt with in the following way:

1   Ask students to match the two parts from each column.
2   Ask students to cover column 2 and remember these parts from the items in column 1.
3   Ask students to cover column 1 and remember these parts from the items in column 2.

Additional activities are:

• Students test each other in pairs.
• Teacher reads out column 1 – students complete with items from column 2, books closed.
• With books closed, students write as many of the items as they can remember.

Ordering

Several different kinds of linguistic element can be given out of order for students to arrange correctly. The ability to put things in the correct order strongly indicates comprehension of the items.

This type of activity is sometimes given before students listen; the first listening task is then to check the order. To make the exercise more enjoyable, and slightly easier, it is a good idea to photocopy the items (or write them out again) and cut them into strips or single words. Students can then physically move the items and try different ordering. The teacher can even make a blackboard / whiteboard set of sentences and encourage students to arrange or direct the arrangement of the items on the board.

Tables and charts

Students are often asked to transfer information into a table by ticking the correct box, or writing notes or single words in the boxes. This activity is a good way of testing comprehension of listening, as it does not require much linguistic output from the students at a time when they should be concentrating on comprehension. Once the table has been completed, it can form the basis of:

1 a checking activity – students compare their tables, and note and discuss differences;

2 a reconstruction activity – students give the information in the table in full, in speech or writing.

The second should be used with caution, bearing in mind the focus on the listening skill in the course rather than on written or spoken production.

Error correction

It was once thought that showing students an error reinforced the error – the students would be even more likely to make that error in the future. We now know that recognising errors is a vital part of language learning. Rather than reinforcing the error, showing it can serve to highlight the problem much better than any number of explanatory words. Students must be able to recognise errors – principally in their own work – and correct them. For this reason, error recognition and correction activities are occasionally used.

Methodology points

Setting up tasks

The teaching notes for many activities begin with the word: 'Set ...'

This single word covers a number of vital functions for the teacher, as follows:

1 Refer students to the rubric – or instructions.

2 Check that they understand **what** to do – get one or two students to explain the task in their own words.

3 Tell the students **how** they are to do the task, if this is not clear in the rubric – as individual work, pairwork, or in groups.

4 Go through the example if there is one. If not, make it clear what the target output is – full sentences, short answers, notes, etc.

5 Go through one or two of the actual prompts, working with a good student to elicit the required output.

Use of visuals

There is a large amount of visual material in the book. This should be exploited in a number of ways:

1 before an activity, to orientate the students, to get them thinking about the situation or the activity, and to provide an opportunity for a small amount of pre-teaching of vocabulary;

2 during the activity, to remind students of important language;

3 after the activity, to help with related work or to revise the target language.

Pronunciation

The focus of this listening course is on a receptive skill rather than a productive one. Therefore, pronunciation of individual phonemes is not focused on directly in the book. However, it is important that students can hear all the target items correctly. In addition, it is arguable that saying a phoneme helps with ear training, therefore some practice of the pronunciation may be desirable.

Comparing answers in pairs

This activity is suggested on almost every occasion when the students have completed an activity individually. This provides all students with a chance to give and explain their answers, which is not possible if the teacher immediately goes through the answers with the whole class.

Monitoring

Pairwork and group activities are, of course, an opportunity for the students to produce spoken language. As mentioned above, this is not the main focus of this course. But the second benefit of these interactional patterns is that they provide an opportunity for the teacher to check three points:

1   that the students are performing the correct task, in the correct way;

2   that the students understand the language of the task they are performing;

3   the elements that need to be covered again for the benefit of the whole class, and the points that need to be dealt with on an individual basis with particular students.

Feedback

At the end of each activity, there should be a feedback stage. During this stage, the correct answers (or a model answer in the case of freer activities) are given, alternative correct answers (if any) are accepted, and wrong answers are discussed. Note: If no answers are provided, answers depend on students.

Feedback can be:

a   high-speed, whole-class, oral – this method is suitable for cases where short answers with no possible variations are required;

b   individual, oral – this method is suitable where answers are longer and / or where variations are possible;

c   individual, on to the board – this method is suitable when the teacher will want to look closely at the correct answers to highlight points of interest or confusion.

Remember – learning does not usually take place when a student gets something right. Learning generally takes place after a student has got something wrong, and begins to understand why it is wrong.

Confirmation and correction

Many activities benefit from a learning tension, i.e., a period of time when students are not sure whether something is right or wrong. The advantages of this tension are:

a   a chance for all students to become involved in an activity before the correct answers are given;

b   a higher level of concentration from students – (tension is quite enjoyable!);

c   a greater focus on the item as students wait for the correct answer;

d   a greater involvement in the process – students become committed to their answers and want to know if they are right and, if not, why not.

In cases where learning tension of this type is desirable, the detailed teacher's notes say: 'Do not confirm or correct (at this point).'

Highlighting grammar

As explained earlier in this introduction, this course is not organised on a grammatical syllabus and does not focus on grammar specifically. However, on occasion, the expression *Highlight the grammar* is used in the teacher's notes. This expression means:

1   focus the students' attention on the grammar point, e.g., *Look at the verb in the first sentence;*

2   write an example of the target grammar on the board;

3   ask a student to read out the sentence / phrase;

4   demonstrate the grammar point in an appropriate way (see below);

5   refer to the board throughout the activity if students are making mistakes.

Ways of dealing with different kinds of grammar point:

- for **word order**, show the order of items in the sentence by numbering them, e.g.,:

1	2	3	4
They	often	have	a special party.

- for **paradigms**, show the changes with different persons of the verb.

I	go
He	go **es**

Self-checking

On a few occasions during the course, the teacher's notes encourage you to ask the students to check their own work. This can be done by referring students to the full tapescript at the end of the book. This is an excellent way to develop the students' recognition and correction of error. Listening, in particular, obviously happens inside someone's head – in the end, each student has to understand his or her *own* error or misunderstanding.

Many of the Language and culture notes in this edition are written for students whose first language is Arabic. If you have students from a different language group, check with the skillsinenglish.com website to see if there are relevant notes. We are constantly increasing the range of languages covered.

Lesson 1: Vocabulary

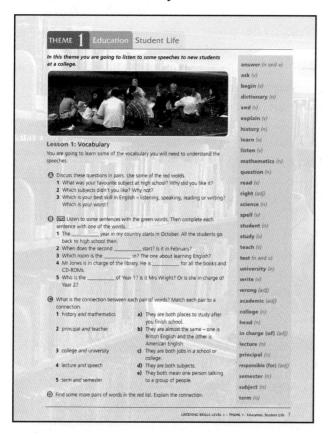

test, end, spell = /e/
read, teach = /iː/
history, begin, explain = /ɪ/ at the beginning
write, right = homophones

Write the following words on the board and tell the students they all have something in common: *answer, history, listen, mathematics, right, write, wrong.* Ask them if they can say what they have in common (all have at least one silent letter). Continue until someone gets it. Keep saying the words to help them; if no one gets the right answer, start saying the words wrongly – i.e., pronouncing the silent letter.

Write 1 and 2 on the board and the words *answer* and *begin* underneath the numbers; exaggerate the stress – on the first syllable and the second syllable respectively. Say more red words and ask if each is like 1 or like 2; add the word to the correct column when everyone has had a chance to think about it. At the end, the board should look like this:

1	2
'answer	be'gin
listen	explain
history	
student	
science	
question	
study	

Don't drill the words – save that for the speaking module; remember, the focus is on listening and hearing salient features.

Exercise A

Set the task. Monitor to see if students are getting anything out of the questions. Feed back with the whole class.

Exercise B

Direct students' attention to the green words. With a weaker class, say the words in isolation first; do not

The background vocabulary – the red words – for all four skills areas is the same in each theme. However, the focus in each skills module should match the skill focus. So, in this listening module, the focus should be on students being able to understand the words in spoken form, in isolation and in context. Give students as much listening practice as possible in this lesson. It is not so important that they should actually say the words – that is why there are no listen and repeat exercises.

Introduction

Before doing Exercise A, highlight some of the key aural points about the red words. For example:

- Say red words in isolation at random. Students find and point to the words in the list.
- Say sentences containing some of the red words. Students find and point to the words in the list.
- Say pairs or groups of words that share sounds. Get students to identify the sounds, e.g.,

ask, answer = /ɑː/

Language and culture note

At first sight, listening and pointing might seem like a primary school activity. In fact, it is a challenging task at any level for any student, because in English the relationship between sound and sight – the spoken and the written word – is complex. It is especially challenging for Arabs because Arabic is largely a phonemic language, which means once you know the sound that a letter makes, you can pronounce an unknown word accurately. Arabs naturally think this is a universal and look to be able to find the same simple relationships in English. But English is not a phonemic language and it is impossible to be sure how an unknown word will be pronounced. This course therefore contains a lot of work on the sound–sight relationship, pointing out patterns (not rules) and exceptions.

ask students to repeat. Then play the recording. With a stronger class, go straight to the recording. Students listen and identify the missing word.

This activity trains students in the vital listening skill of picking out unknown words from the stream of speech.

Having identified the missing set of sounds, they then try to find the correct word or phrase in the green list. This helps to train aural memory – the ability to hold meaningless sounds in the brain until one is able to match them to a 'picture' – the written form.

Students complete the task individually, then check in pairs. Play each sentence several times if students are struggling to pick out the new words. Feed back with the whole class and deal with the meaning of the words.

Answers
1   The <u>academic</u> year in my country starts in October. All the students go back to high school then.
2   When does the second <u>term</u> start? Is it in February?
3   Which room is the <u>lecture</u> in? The one about learning English?

4   Mr Jones is in charge of the library. He is <u>responsible</u> for all the books and CD-ROMs.
5   Who is the <u>head</u> of Year 1? Is it Mrs Wright? Or is she in charge of Year 2?

Exercise C

Most of the work so far has been on listening. The focus now moves to meaning. We remember new information when we can connect it with known information. This activity helps students to make such connections.

Answers
1   d) They are both subjects.
2   c) They are both jobs in a school or college.
3   a) They are both places to study after you finish school.
4   e) They both mean one person talking to a group of people.
5   b) They are almost the same – one is British English and the other is American English.

Exercise D

Demonstrate how you can do this and teach them different ways to connect items, e.g.,
* opposites / converses – *ask* and *answer*
* synonyms / almost the same – *study* and *learn*
* verb / noun – *study* and *student*
* collocation – you can either use this word or say that some words often go together, e.g., *ask a question*

Answers
Possible pairs:

ask and *answer*	*teach* and *test*
begin and *end*	*teach* and *learn*
read and *write*	*right* and *wrong*

Closure

Say the words from the green list and get students to mark the stress.

Lesson 2: Listening

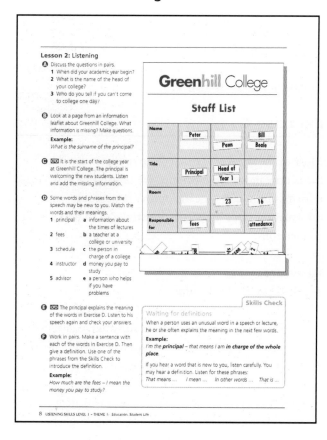

Exercise A

This is further practice of the target words – from the point of view of meaning this time. Set for pairwork. Feed back with the whole class.

Exercise B

Refer students to the illustration. Make sure students understand what this text is. Work through a couple of the questions, then set for pairwork. Feed back with the whole class. Don't deal with any of the new words – this is the target of the activity in Exercise D. It is vital that students always have a task to do while they are listening. We rarely if ever listen without a purpose.

Answers
Possible questions:
What is the surname of the principal?
Which room is the principal in? / What is the number of the principal's room?
What is the first name of the head of Year 1?
What is the head of Year 1 responsible for?
What is the title of Bill Beale?

Exercise C

Make sure students understand the scenario and that they are looking at the Staff List during the first listening. Play the recording, twice if necessary. Give students plenty of time to fill in the missing information and compare in pairs. Feed back, building up the Staff List on the board.

Note that the names of the people are examples of the target phonemes from the next lesson – i.e., /p/ vs. /b/ and /ɪ/ vs /iː/. Insist therefore on good pronunciation of the names during the feedback, as this will begin the highlighting of these sounds. It is impossible to get inside someone's head to adjust their perception of a sound, but it has been found that trying to produce a sound improves ability to perceive it in speech.

Introduction

Revise vocabulary from Lesson 1, especially the green words. Say the beginning of one of the words and get students to complete the word. This is practice in the vital skill of predicting words from the first one or two phonemes – this is the skill that enables native speakers to understand speech that is actually being produced faster than the brain can process all the aural stimuli. We therefore sample – i.e., listen to some sounds and predict the remainder while we skip on to the next section.

Methodology note

You know your students better than anybody, certainly better than the writer of this course. Listen to each lecture while you are preparing your lesson and decide if you need to pre-teach some more words. Clearly, you should not pre-teach words which are the target of listening activities, but you may well feel that other words in the text will cause students to stumble and thus need pre-teaching.

Answers

Name	Title	Room	Responsible for
Peter Bean	Principal	15	fees
Polly Penn	Head of Yr 1	23	schedule
Bill Beale	Registrar	16	attendance

Language and culture note

Take every opportunity to move out of the 'teacher as knower' role that Arab students are familiar with. The course provides sources of information other than the teacher and it is important that you should not pre-empt the use of these sources. In this case, the principal's speech contains definitions of the words in Exercise D (which are also the presumed new words on the Staff List). Provided you do not explain the words when the students first encounter them, they will be forced to try to hear the definitions in the principal's speech.

Exercise D

Set the task for individual completion and pairwork checking, but do not confirm or correct at this stage (see the Language and culture note above). There are two other words that may be new to students – *attendance* and *staff*. The meanings are not given directly in definitions but can be inferred from other things that the principal says, i.e., *attendance* = going to college; *staff* = people who work at the college (or anywhere).

Exercise E

Play the recording, pausing after each definition for students to check their own work. Feed back, using the two-column activity approach.

Refer students to the Skills Check, which shows them the kinds of word and phrase that are used to introduce spoken definitions. Note that this sort of information is vital if we are to understand spoken language. There is not time for the brain to decode each individual word into meaning, then assemble the words into phrases, and then look up the meaning of the phrase. We must 'chunk' phrases so that the brain can immediately

identify the purpose and move on to listening to the next bit. For example, if you hear *That means* and you already understand what the word in question means, you can ignore or only sample the next few words.

Answers

1	principal	c	the person in charge of a college
2	fees	d	money you pay to study
3	schedule	a	information about the times of lectures
4	instructor	b	a teacher at a college or university
5	advisor	e	a person who helps if you have problems

Exercise F

Give several examples, and build them up on the board. Then set for pairwork. Monitor. Feed back by eliciting good examples from several pairs.

Closure

Go through the information in the Staff List, making mistakes. The mistakes should focus on sounds rather than content. Students have to stop you and correct you, e.g.,

Teacher: So, the name of the principal is Peter Benn.

Student: No, it's Peter Bean.

Play the speech again (track 2 on CD1).

Language and culture note

Throughout this course, the word *college* is used to mean tertiary-level institution. This is a common use of the word in the English-speaking world. The Arabic word *kulia* is almost co-extensive with *college*, i.e., it can mean a faculty or school of a university or an academy of higher learning. However, it can also mean a secondary school, so you will need to stress that in this course *college* is interchangeable with *university* and not with *secondary school*. The fictional Greenhill College is a tertiary establishment with degree-level courses.

Lesson 3: Learning new skills

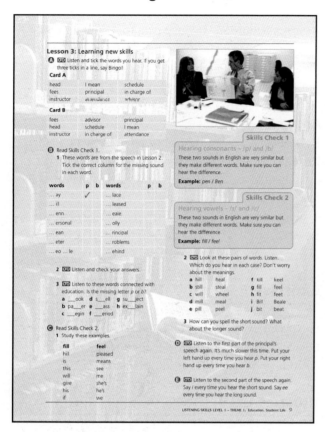

Introduction

Remind students of spoken definitions. Get students to define each of the words or phrases (except *I mean*) in the noughts and crosses grid.

Exercise A

Explain how to play Bingo. Ask students to pick one of the cards – A or B. Point out that both cards have the same words, which are all green words from Lesson 1. They must listen and tick a word when they hear it. If they get three ticks in a line across (not diagonally or downwards), they win. Go through the first word as an example and make sure that students are ticking the correct word in each case. In theory, someone should say 'Bingo!' when you get to *** in the tapescript on page 99 of this Teacher's Book. If not, play the tape again, or read out the sentences with the target words in until someone shouts out.

Exercise B

Remember that the key point in this listening module is *hearing* the difference, so do not spend time making students *produce* the sounds with discrimination.

Refer students to Skills Check 1. Demonstrate the two sounds. Write 1 and 2 on the board and put the two letters representing the phonemes under the numbers. Say each phoneme several times and get students to identify the sound by saying 1 or 2. Repeat with the phonemes at the beginning of words.

1   Set the task for individual completion. Students tick in the appropriate box.
2   Play the recording, pausing after each word if necessary. Feed back by writing the words on the board. Do not force perfect pronunciation – focus on correct identification.
3   This activity checks ability to hear the sounds in other words from this theme. Play the recording with no pre-teaching. Students write in the correct letter. Feed back, getting the words on the board.

Language and culture note

There is no phoneme in Arabic that approximates to /p/ in English. Students will therefore tend to hear all sounds made with the two lips closing and opening as /b/. In fact, in English, the contrast is quite an important one, with many minimal pairs such as *pray* and *bray*, *pie* and *buy*. (A minimal pair is a pair of words where just one phoneme changes the meaning.) By this stage of their learning, your students will know that the two phonemes exist in English, but they will still not be able to distinguish them accurately (or produce /p/, but that is a concern for the Speaking module).

Answers

1 and 2

words	p	b	words	p	b
… ay	✓		… lace	✓	
… ill		✓	… leased	✓	
… enn	✓		… eale		✓
… ersonal	✓		… olly	✓	
… ean		✓	… rincipal	✓	
… eter	✓		… roblems	✓	
… eo … le	✓		… ehind		✓

3 a book   e pass
   b paper   f period
   c begin   g subject
   d spell   h explain

Exercise C

1 Let students study all the examples. Then highlight the difference by exaggerating the vowel sound on each side. Exaggerating is a good highlighting technique for most listening activities.

2 Explain that students are only going to hear one of the words each time. Make it very clear this is just to improve listening – the meaning of the words is not important. Do not teach the meaning of words. But make the point that these words exist in English so you must be able to hear which a speaker is saying. Play the recording for the first two or three and check that the students understand what to do. Complete the activity. Feed back by asking students if they heard /ɪ/ or /iː/.

3 The focus of this module is not on writing and spelling but, as noted, the ability to predict is a key listening sub-skill. Get students to make some predictions about sound–sight relationships.

Answers

2 a hill   f kill
   b steal   g feel
   c will   h feet
   d meal   i Bill
   e pill   j beat

3 From this evidence: short sound = *i*; longer sound = *ea* or *ee*.

Language and culture note 1

The contrast between /ɪ/ and /iː/ exists in Arabic, so students should have no difficulty hearing the two sounds. However, because English is not phonemic, they will not know which of these sounds a particular word will contain. They will also have problems with predicting the sound, and therefore with identifying the word correctly in speech. In particular, they will expect:

• all words with the letter *i* to contain the sound /ɪ/ and this of course is not true (c.f. *live* and *life*);

• a consistent spelling of the sound /iː/ – again not true, as it can been written with *ee, ea, ie,* etc.

Of course, we are not teaching spelling here – that is for the Writing module, but unless you can predict the sound of a word which is familiar to you in writing, you cannot identify it correctly in the split second available to you in the stream of speech.

Language and culture note 2

In Arabic, as noted elsewhere, an unknown word can be accurately sounded out because the language is phonemic. Having tried to do this in English and failed, students at this level have probably given up trying to predict the sound of a new word from its written form because of the apparent insanity of English spelling. However, there are in fact some very useful patterns – not rules – which will enable accurate prediction 90% of the time. The course aims to teach these patterns. You can keep saying this to your students: English spelling is *majnoon* (crazy), but there are some patterns to help you.

Exercises D and E

These give practice in identifying sounds in the stream of speech. Complete the activities as described.

Closure

Ask students to look back at the red words (Lesson 1), find words with one or more the four target phonemes and say each word.

Methodology note

This course does not set out to teach the phonemic script. However, it does show the phonemes where this is useful for pointing up sounds and sound–sight problems. The writer believes that students should learn to recognise (not write) key phonemes in written form so they can use a dictionary more effectively as a tool for predicting the sounds of new words and, in other modules, as a tool for producing sounds correctly.

Lesson 4: Applying new skills

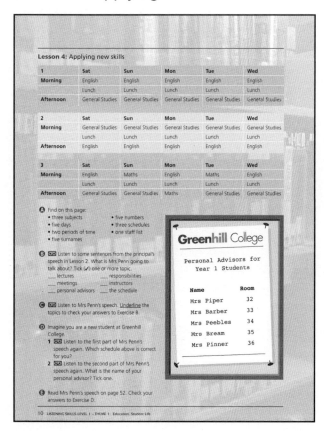

Introduction

Remind students of the broad scenario of this module – new students arriving and hearing about the college and the timetable / schedule.

Exercise A

High-speed oral activity with a fast class. Pair or group work then oral feedback with a slower class.

Answers

• three subjects:	English, Mathematics (Maths), General Studies
• five days:	Saturday to Wednesday
• two periods of time:	morning, afternoon
• five surnames:	Piper, Barber, Peebles, Bream, Pinner
• five numbers:	32 to 36
• three schedules:	1, 2 and 3
• one staff list:	under the schedules

Exercise B

Give students time to read the possible topics. Play the recording with the principal's introduction. Repeat if necessary. Do not feed back at this point.

Exercise C

Play the recording of Mrs Penn's speech. Feed back with the whole class. Play the recording again and get students to identify when the topic changes.

Answers

the schedule; instructors; personal advisors

Methodology note

A key listening skill is predicting content of a lecture / talk from information in the introduction to the talk. In Exercises B and C, the students are encouraged to do just this – predict from the introduction, then check from the talk itself.

Exercise D

It is important that students understand the rubric here – you are a new student at Greenhill College.

1. Refer students to the schedules at the top of the page. Get them to find two differences between 1 and 2 and between 2 and 3. Play the recording. Students complete individually and compare in pairs. Do not confirm or correct at this point.

2. Refer students to the list of staff and work through the information there. Get students to find information quickly through high-speed questions, e.g., *Which room is Mrs Piper in? Who's in Room 36?* Play the recording. Students complete individually and compare in pairs. Do not confirm or correct at this point.

Exercise E

Refer students to the tapescript on page 52.

Answers
1   Timetable 2
2   Answers depend on students, but this is the cross-check:

Surname beginning with	Student advisor
A, B, C, D or E	Mrs Piper
F, G, H, I or J	Mrs Barber
K, L, M, N or O	Mrs Peebles
P, Q, R, S or T	Mrs Bream
U, V, W, X, Y or Z	Mrs Pinner

Methodology note

Personalisation is a key part of most listening activities in this course. As noted above, we rarely listen without having a reason, and unless you give students a specific reason for listening, they are unlikely to bring real-life listening skills to bear on the task. In real life, the students would be sitting in the hall thinking – *Which information here applies to me?* We must try to mimic that situation as closely as possible in order to develop genuine listening skills.

Methodology note

Listening is not the same as reading. Spoken text is ephemeral and can only be accessed directly once. It is a stream, not a set of clearly isolated words for identification. So things that would be easy to understand in written form are incomprehensible in spoken form. We must give students the opportunity to associate the aural memory with the written form, to correctly associate what they hear with what was actually said. Allowing students to read the transcript of spoken text BEFORE feedback on listening activities is therefore a key learning stage.

Closure

General talk about information of the sort imparted to the students in this module. Elicit 'real' information, i.e., *What is your schedule? Who is the principal / head / student advisor? Which room do you have lectures / classes in,* etc.

Play the speech again (track 11 on CD1).

Lesson 1: Vocabulary

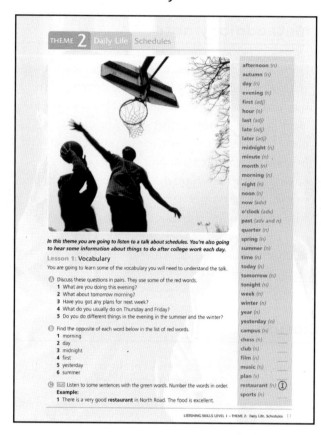

THEME **2** Daily Life | Schedules

In this theme you are going to listen to a talk about schedules. You're also going to hear some information about things to do after college work each day.

Lesson 1: Vocabulary
You are going to learn some of the vocabulary you will need to understand the talk.

Ⓐ Discuss these questions in pairs. They use some of the red words.
1 What are you doing this evening?
2 What about tomorrow morning?
3 Have you got any plans for next week?
4 What do you usually do on Thursday and Friday?
5 Do you do different things in the evening in the summer and the winter?

Ⓑ Find the opposite of each word below in the list of red words.
1 morning
2 day
3 midnight
4 first
5 yesterday
6 summer

Ⓒ Listen to some sentences with the green words. Number the words in order.
Example:
1 There is a very good **restaurant** in North Road. The food is excellent.

afternoon (n)
autumn (n)
day (n)
evening (n)
first (adj)
hour (n)
last (adj)
late (adj)
later (adj)
midnight (n)
minute (n)
month (n)
morning (n)
night (n)
noon (n)
now (adv)
o'clock (adv)
past (adv and n)
quarter (n)
spring (n)
summer (n)
time (n)
today (n)
tomorrow (n)
tonight (n)
week (n)
winter (n)
year (n)
yesterday (n)
campus (n)
chess (n)
club (n)
film (n)
music (n)
plan (v)
restaurant (n)
sports (n)

LISTENING SKILLS LEVEL 1 – THEME 2: Daily Life, Schedules

Introduction

Write the theme title and subtitle on the board. Say the words and elicit / teach the meanings.

Exercise A

Divide the class into pairs to discuss the questions. Feed back with the whole class.

Set the activity again; this time ask students to substitute the red words in each question with a different red word from the list.

Exercise B

Set the task for students to complete individually. Elicit answers.

Answers
1 afternoon
2 night
3 noon
4 last
5 tomorrow
6 winter

Extra activities

1 Students put the words into logical groups, e.g.,
   seasons: *autumn, winter, summer, spring*
   time phrases: *today, tomorrow, last week*

2 Say sentences aloud for students to complete with a word from the list, e.g.,
   Teacher: I can't mark your work now but I'll look at it …
   Students: *later / tomorrow.*
   Teacher: In England, January is usually the coldest …
   Students: *month.*
   Teacher: We don't usually say twelve o'clock at night, we say …
   Students: *midnight.*

Exercise C

Direct students' attention to the green words. With a weak class, say the words in isolation first; do not ask students to repeat. Then play the recording. With a stronger class, go straight to the recording.

Check students understand the task and go over the example with them. Play each sentence, several times if necessary. Pause after each sentence for students to write their answer. Students should complete this individually and only compare answers when all sentences have been played.

Elicit answers and replay any sentences that caused difficulty. Finish by allowing the students to read the sentences in the tapescript and listen to them at the same time.

Answers

1 restaurant
2 chess
3 sports
4 music
5 club
6 campus
7 plan
8 film

Methodology note

There is a huge difference between identifying a word in isolation and picking the same word out from the stream of speech. Always try to contextualise words that you want students to be able to hear in speech, otherwise you are giving them false confidence. Always give students an opportunity to see the words they are hearing so they can associate sound and sight effectively.

Extra activities

1 Remind students of the minimal pair work they did in Theme 1 Lesson 3 on /ɪ/ and /iː/ sounds (*mill, meal*, etc). Ask them to find words in the red and green lists with these sounds:

/ɪ/ = m_i_dnight, m_i_nute, spr_i_ng, w_i_nter, f_i_lm, mus_i_c, even_i_ng
/iː/ = _e_vening, w_ee_k,

2 Which words spelt with the letter *i* do not have either of these sounds?

f_i_rst, n_i_ght, ton_i_ght, midn_i_ght

Closure

Practise briefly (more will be done in the speaking section) the pronunciation of the green words. Then ask students to make a sentence with each word.

Lesson 2: Listening

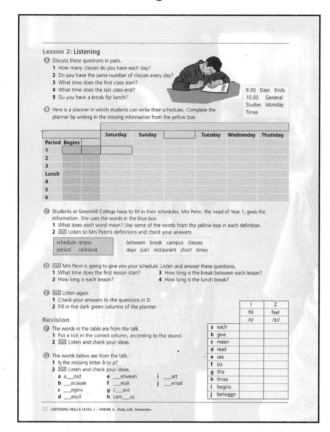

Introduction

If necessary, spend a few minutes revising telling the time, making sure students can do it accurately.

Language and culture note

There are some similarities and some differences between the British English and Arabic forms of spoken time. You might find it useful to compare some of the forms.

English	Arabic
It is four o'clock.	the time fourth
It is five past four.	the time fourth and five
It is quarter past four.	the time fourth and a quarter
It is half past four.	the time fourth and a half
It is twenty five to five.	the time fifth except five and twenty
It is quarter to five.	the time fifth except a quarter
It is ten to five.	the time five except ten

Exercise A

This exercise could be used as an opportunity to highlight and revise simple present question forms. Practise some of the questions with the class, focussing on the unstressed words *do* and *does*.

Divide the class into pairs for question and answer practice. Elicit some of their answers and check again that students are saying times correctly.

Exercise B

Give students time to read and take in all the information, then set the task. If possible, use an OHT of the schedule on the board to help you explain.

Students complete individually then compare answers. Elicit answers using the OHT on the board, if possible.

Answers

Times	Days
Ends	Monday
9.00 10.00	General Studies

Exercise C

Give students time to read the instructions carefully. Say the four words so that students can recognise them in context. Do the definition of the first word with the class as an example.

Students complete the remaining three words; do not confirm or correct at this stage.

Play the recording for students to check their definitions. Pause the recording after each definition and write it on the board.

Answers

schedule	the days and times of classes
period	a part of the day
recess	a short break between classes
cafeteria	the restaurant on the campus

Exercise D

Set the task. Play the recording. Students complete individually then compare answers. Do not confirm or correct at this stage.

Exercise E

Play the recording again. Have students check their answers from Exercise D.

Answers
1   9.00.
2   One hour.
3   10 minutes.

Set the second task. Play the recording. If you like, pause after each relevant section of the tapescript. Replay as necessary. Note: You can fill in all the times from the information given, but students may need to hear the key information several times.

Elicit full answers in order to focus on accuracy, e.g.,

Teacher: What time does lunch begin?

Students: It begins at twenty past twelve. (etc.)

Answers

Period	Begins	Ends
1	9.00	10.00
2	10.10	11.10
3	11.20	12.20
Lunch	12.20	1.20
4	1.20	2.20
5	2.30	3.30
6	3.40	4.40

Extra activity

Students can now read the listening text on page 53 of their books while you play the recording again.

Exercise F

1   Do the first answer with the class as an example. Students complete individually.
2   Play the recording, then students compare answers. Elicit answers and practise pronunciation.

Answers

		1 fill /ɪ/	2 feel /iː/
a	each		✓
b	give	✓	
c	mean		✓
d	read		✓
e	see		✓
f	six	✓	
g	this	✓	
h	three		✓
i	begins	✓	
j	between		✓

Exercise G

1   Set the task. Students complete individually.
2   Play the recording. Students compare answers. Elicit answers and practise pronunciation of each word. Ask students to make sentences using some of the words.

Answers

b	p
about	pencil
because	space
begins	campus
between	part
break	period

Closure

Dictate some of the key words from this theme so far.

Lesson 3: Learning new skills

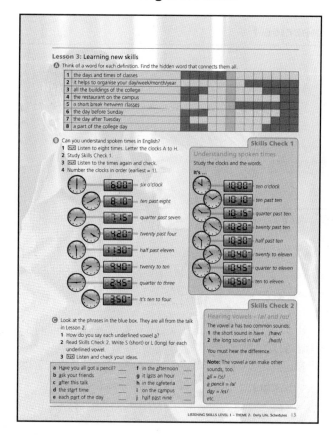

Methodology note

This is, fundamentally, a listening course. Therefore, arguably, there should be no activities that involve reading and writing, as word puzzles do. However, there is some research to suggest that people need to get a visual representation even of spoken language in order to be able to remember it. In addition, this course sets out to teach key words from a range of lexical sets, and one way to improve retention of vocabulary is to recycle it in many different ways. So those are two good arguments for the crosswords that are often the first activity of Lesson 3. That said, do not spend ages on the spelling of words here. The key learning task is matching the definitions and the items. The crossword format simply makes it a bit more fun – if, of course, you like crosswords.

Introduction

Explain to students that this is the lesson where they generally learn new listening skills. They then apply these skills in the next lesson.

Exercise A

Set for pairwork. Demonstrate how students must think of the correct word and then try to remember the spelling in order to fit the word into the space. Since all the words have appeared in the first two lessons, they should be able to find them somewhere in the theme to date and copy the spelling. Feed back, ideally onto an OHT of the puzzle blank. They may not be able to dictate the spelling of the words, since they have not yet learnt the correct pronunciation of English letter names, but this could be done as a deep-end strategy, in preparation for this learning task in Theme 5.

Exercise B

1   Set for individual work then pairwork checking. Play the recording, pausing after each one. Do not feed back.

2   Set for individual work then pairwork checking.

3   Play the recording again. Feed back, ideally with an OHT of the clock and watch faces. Point out the use of special words: *quarter*, *half*, *past* and *to*.

4   Set for pairwork. Feed back onto the board or an OHT. Note that this is quite a challenging activity, although made less so because there are no times with the same hour.

Answers

1–3 Here is the order on the recording:

c	6.00	six o'clock
f	8.10	ten past eight
b	7.15	quarter past seven
d	4.20	twenty past four
g	11.30	half past eleven
a	9.40	twenty to ten
h	2.45	quarter to three
e	3.50	It's ten to four.

4   Here is the chronological order:

    h 2.45   quarter to three
    e 3.50   It's ten to four.
    d 4.20   twenty past four
    c 6.00   six o'clock
    b 7.15   quarter past seven
    f 8.10   ten past eight
    a 9.40   twenty to ten
    g 11.30   half past eleven

Methodology note

Even native-speaker children are having growing difficulty in telling the time from an analogue clock, given the increasing use of digital format. I certainly do not think it is the job of a language course to teach analogue time if it is not known in the students' L1. Everything on this page is, therefore, printed in both analogue and digital.

Exercise C

1   Give students time to read through the 10 phrases and allow brief discussion with their partners. Do not elicit answers at this stage – tell students you will come back to it.

2   Students read Skills Check 2. Allow them to discuss the questions in pairs. Elicit answers, but do not confirm or correct.

3   Play the recording. Feed back orally.

Answers

		short	long	notes
a	have	✓		this could be schwa, but is less common in questions
b	ask		✓	
c	after		✓	
d	start		✓	
e	part		✓	
f	lasts		✓	
g	cafeteria	✓		the final *a* has the schwa sound, of course
h	campus	✓		
i	half		✓	
j	past		✓	

Closure

Dictate some times for students to write down in digital form.

Lesson 4: Applying new skills

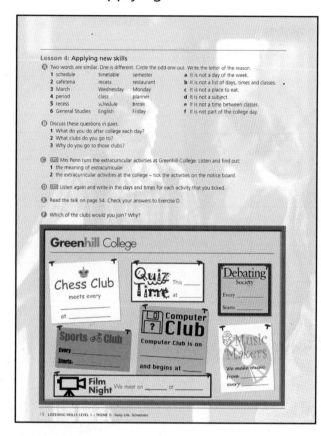

Lesson 4: Applying new skills

Ⓐ Two words are similar. One is different. Circle the odd one out. Write the letter of the reason.
1	schedule	timetable	semester	a It is not a day of the week.
2	cafeteria	recess	restaurant	b It is not a list of days, times and classes.
3	March	Wednesday	Monday	c It is not a place to eat.
4	period	class	planner	d It is not a subject.
5	recess	schedule	break	e It is not a time between classes.
6	General Studies	English	Friday	f It is not part of the college day.

Ⓑ Discuss these questions in pairs.
1 What do you do after college each day?
2 What clubs do you go to?
3 Why do you go to those clubs?

Ⓒ ▦ Mrs Penn runs the extracurricular activities at Greenhill College. Listen and find out:
1 the meaning of extracurricular.
2 the extracurricular activities at the college – tick the activities on the notice board.

Ⓓ ▦ Listen again and write in the days and times for each activity that you ticked.

Ⓔ Read the talk on page 54. Check your answers to Exercise D.

Ⓕ Which of the clubs would you join? Why?

Greenhill College

Chess Club
meets every
____
at ____

Quiz Time
This ____
at ____

Debating Society
Every ____
Starts ____

Sports Club
Every ____
Starts: ____

Computer Club
Computer Club is on ____
and begins at ____

Music Makers
We make music from ____ every ____

Film Night
We meet on ____ at ____

14 LISTENING SKILLS LEVEL 1 – THEME 2: Daily Life, Schedules

Introduction

Point out that this is the lesson in each theme where they apply the new skills learnt in Lesson 3.

Ask students to tell you what the new skills are this time. Refer them back to the Skills Check when they start to falter.

Methodology note

Students should be encouraged to use the Skills Checks as a reference tool – i.e., they go back and look at the Skills Checks again from time to time when they need to remind themselves of a point. This is why the checks are all in the same coloured boxes and normally on the outer side of the second right page of the theme.

Exercise A

This is a revision exercise. Set the task. Make sure students realise that this is about meaning, not form or sound. Students complete individually then compare answers. Elicit answers and correct any mispronounced words.

Answers

1	semester	b	It is not a list of days, times and classes.
2	recess	c	It is not a place to eat.
3	March	a	It is not a day of the week.
4	planner	f	It is not part of the college day.
5	schedule	e	It is not a time between classes.
6	Friday	d	It is not a subject.

Exercise B

Give students time to read the questions. Elicit some ideas for possible answers and check students use the simple present tense accurately.

Students practise the questions and answers in pairs.

Exercise C

Set the tasks. Play the recording. Elicit answers. Discuss what kinds of activities might take place in each club.

Answers

1 The extra things you can do after college work.
2 The following should be ticked:
Sports Club
Film Night
Quiz Time
Computer Club
Music Makers

Exercise D

Set the task. Play the recording. Students complete the task individually. While you rewind the recording for another chance to listen, students can compare answers. Play the recording again. Do not confirm or correct at this point.

Exercise E

Students can read the talk silently or can follow the talk while you play the recording once more. Elicit answers.

Answers
Saturday
8.00 Sports Club

Sunday
8.30 Film Night

Monday
7.45 Quiz Time

Tuesday
8.15 Computer Club

Wednesday
7.30 Music Makers

Exercise F

Students discuss in pairs. Elicit some of their ideas.

Closure

1   Give students two minutes to ask you about any other words or expressions in the talk that might be new to them.
2   Spend a few minutes focussing on one or two of the following language areas from the talk. Use the tapescript in the back of the book or an OHT of it.
      sequencers: *first, then, finally*
      imperative used as an invitation: *come with ... come and learn ...*
      prepositions: *on Sunday, at 8.15*
      conditionals: *If you want ... If you play ...*

Lesson 1: Vocabulary

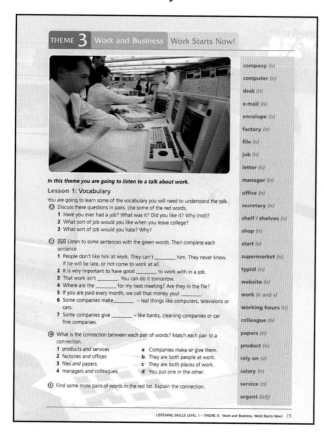

Introduction

Write the title of the lesson on the board and exploit the visual. You should certainly be able to elicit some of the red words.

Exercise A

Set the task. Students discuss in pairs. Monitor and note which students have used some of the red words in interesting or useful sentences. Elicit some of these sentences at the end of the activity for the whole class to hear.

Try some of the *point and say* activities suggested in Theme 1 Lesson 1 Introduction.

Exercise B

Say the green words, but don't ask students to repeat them. Give students time to read the sentences. Play the recording, twice if necessary.

Students complete individually then compare answers. Elicit answers. Ask further questions to check comprehension of each word.

Answers

1 People don't like him at work. They can't <u>rely on</u> him. They never know if he will be late – or not come to work at all.
2 It is very important to have good <u>colleagues</u> to work with in a job.
3 That work isn't <u>urgent</u>. You can do it tomorrow.
4 Where are the <u>papers</u> for my next meeting? Are they in the file?
5 If you are paid every month, we call that money your <u>salary</u>.
6 Some companies make <u>products</u> – real things like computers, televisions or cars.
7 Some companies give <u>services</u> – like banks, cleaning companies or car hire companies.

Exercise C

Students complete in pairs. Elicit answers. This is a two-column activity, therefore it lends itself to further exploitation. For example (books closed):
a say the left column, students give you the right column;
b say the right column, students give you the left column;
c students test each other in pairs.

Answers

1 products and services   a Companies make or give them.

2 factories and offices   c They are both places of work.

3 files and papers   d You put one in the
                             other.

4 managers and   b They are both people
   colleagues   at work.

Exercise D

Students complete in pairs. Elicit answers and insist on
full, accurate sentences to explain the connection:
> *You put a letter in an envelope.*
> *They are both places you buy things from.*

Answers
Answers depend on students, but some possible
examples are:
envelope – letter
company – manager
website – e-mail
shop – supermarket

Closure

1 Refer to the visual again. Elicit some of the green
   words: you can certainly see *papers* and the people
   are presumably giving a *service*. The people at the
   desk are *colleagues* but the man standing up on the
   left may be a *manager*. You can ask why the
   company *relies on* these people; perhaps they are
   controlling something – electricity production?

2 Put some of the green words in context for
   students to identify – see Theme 2 Lesson 1.
   OR
   Make sentences that should end with a green word,
   e.g.,
   > The working hours are very long but the job has
   > a very good *salary*.
   > This is Andrew, one of my *colleagues*.
   > He is someone you can really *rely on*.
   > You must do this work today. It's really *urgent*.

Lesson 2: Listening

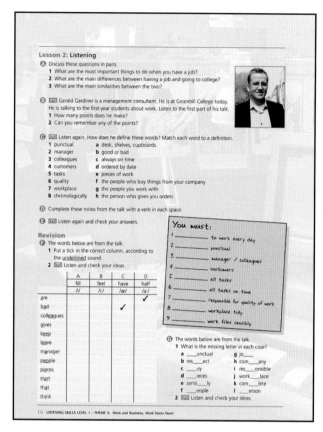

Introduction

Revise the green words from the previous lesson. Dictate some of them.

Exercise A

Revise / teach the antonyms *difference* and *similarity*. Teach the plurals and elicit the adjectives *different* and *similar*.

Students read the questions for the activity. Elicit one example idea for each question from the class. Then students think of further ideas in pairs. Elicit some of their ideas.

Exercise B

Students read the instructions. Check understanding: *What does Gerald do? Where is he today?* Pre-teach the word *respect* (*v*).

Set the task, and play the recording. Students complete individually, then compare answers. Elicit the answer to the first question.

Write the numbers 1–9 on the board in a list. Elicit any points students may have remembered. Write them in note form next to the appropriate number. It is unlikely students will have understood or remembered all the points from one playing. So play the recording again and see how many more points students can add to the list. When you have elicited all the points, erase the list so as not to pre-empt Exercises D and E.

Answers

1   He makes nine points. (Pre-organisers / signpost words are highlighted later.)

Exercise C

Give students time to try the exercise before you play the recording again. Then play the recording for students to check their answers.

Elicit answers and practise pronunciation of the vocabulary if you wish (but see Exercise F).

Answers

1	punctual	c	always on time
2	manager	h	the person who gives you orders
3	colleagues	g	the people you work with
4	customers	f	the people who buy things from your company
5	tasks	e	pieces of work
6	quality	b	good or bad
7	workplace	a	desk, shelves, cupboards
8	chronologically	d	ordered by date

Exercise D

Students complete individually then compare answers. Do not confirm or correct at this point.

Exercise E

Play the recording and elicit answers. Check the correct form of the verb has been used each time, as well as pronunciation. Ask students to spell some of the verbs: *complete, respect, organise.*

At this point, you may choose to play the recording one last time with the students following in their books (page 54). Alternatively, you may prefer to do this after Exercise G. In either case, you may wish to focus on one or two language points, including:

> defining / explaining: *that means … that is … in other words …*
> imperatives for advice: *change … think …*

Answers

1 go to work every day
2 be punctual
3 respect manager / colleagues
4 respect customers
5 do all tasks
6 complete all tasks on time
7 be responsible for quality of work
8 keep workplace tidy
9 organise work files sensibly

Exercise F

See how many words containing each sound students can remember from Themes 1 and 2.
1 Set the task for students to complete individually.
2 Play the recording. Students compare answers. Elicit answers and practise pronunciation.

Answers

	A fill /ɪ/	B feel /iː/	C have /æ/	D half /ɑː/
are				✓
bad			✓	
colleagues		✓		
gives	✓			
keep		✓		
leave		✓		
manager			✓	
people		✓		
pieces		✓		
start				✓
that			✓	
think	✓			

Exercise G

1 Set the task for students to complete individually.
2 Play the recording. Students compare answers. Elicit answers and practise pronunciation.

Answers

a punctual
b respect
c buy
d pieces
e sensibly
f people
g job
h company
i responsible
j workplace
k complete
l person

Closure

Redo Exercise C using some of the two-column activities.

Play the talk again (track 25 on CD1)

Lesson 3: Learning new skills

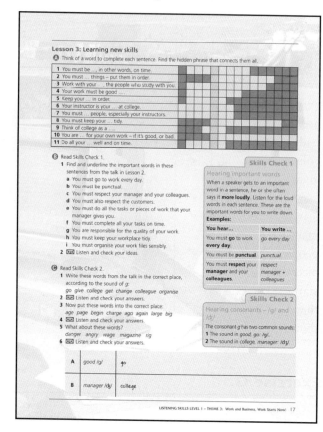

Introduction

Use Exercise A as an introduction to the lesson. This is basically a revision of meaning and spelling activity. When you elicit answers, you can also revise pronunciation from the point of view of identification of the word in context.

Answers

1	P	U	N	C	T	U	A	L			
2					O	R	G	A	N	I	S	E
3	C	O	L	L	E	A	G	U	E	S	
4	Q	U	A	L	I	T	Y				
5	F	I	L	E	S						
6	M	A	N	A	G	E	R				
7	R	E	S	P	E	C	T				
8			W	O	R	K	P	L	A	C	E	
9		J	O	B							
10			R	E	S	P	O	N	S	I	B	L	E
11	T	A	S	K	S						

Exercise B

This is an introduction to taking notes.

Remind students of the talk they listened to by Mr Gardiner in Lesson 2. Read Skills Check 1 aloud with the students following in their books – make sure you stress the words in the examples correctly!

1   Set task 1 for students to complete individually. Do not elicit answers but monitor to check students have got the right idea.

2   Play the recording. Students compare answers. Play the recording again if necessary. Elicit answers and write the notes ('important words') on the board.

Answers

Possible answers:

a   You must go to work <u>every day</u>.

b   You must be <u>punctual</u>.

c   You must <u>respect</u> your <u>manager</u> and your <u>colleagues</u>.

d   You must also <u>respect</u> the <u>customers</u>.

e   You must do all the <u>tasks</u> or pieces of work that your manager gives you.

f   You must <u>complete</u> all your tasks <u>on time</u>.

g   You are responsible for the <u>quality</u> of your work.

h   You must keep your <u>workplace</u> <u>tidy</u>.

i   You must <u>organise</u> your work files sensibly.

Exercise C

1   Read Skills Check 2 aloud with the students following in their books. Check students understand the task and go over the examples with them. Students complete individually.

2   Play the recording, and repeat if necessary. Students compare answers. Elicit answers. Practise pronunciation.

3 and 4 Repeat the above procedures.

5 and 6 Repeat the above procedures.

Ask students to choose (or you can allocate if you prefer) any three words from the activity; they should write a sentence for each one.

Monitor to see which students have written something interesting. Ask these students to read out their sentences. Practise these sentences with the class.

Language and culture note

Arab speakers have a particular problem with these two sounds. Arabic only has one sound to cover these two – in some varieties of Arabic, /g/ is used, in others /dʒ/. Ask students how they pronounce the *jeem / geem* letter in Arabic to find out their own variety – e.g., the first sound in the word for university – *jamaa* or *gamaa*. Point out that both sounds exist in all varieties of English but sometimes *g* is pronounced one way, sometimes the other.

Although this activity is about pronunciation of *g*, you might like to deal here with the fact that *j* is always pronounced as /dʒ/, e.g., *jam, just, June, July, jump, major.*

Closure

Ask students if they can see any pattern in the pronunciation of *g* as /dʒ/. They should notice that the letter *e* comes after every occurrence. This might not be a 100% rule but it is a powerful pattern.

Answers

A	B
good	manager
/g/	/dʒ/
go	college
give	change
get	age
colleague	page
organise	charge
begin	large
ago	danger
again	wage
big	
angry	
magazine	
rig	

Lesson 4: Applying new skills

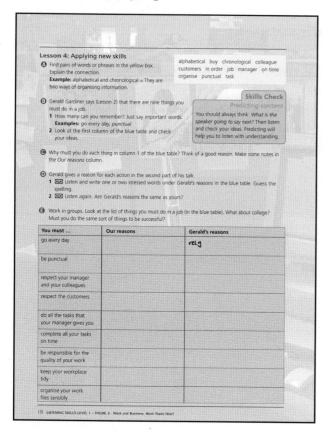

Introduction

Say each of the words / phrases in the yellow box, stressing each one very strongly in a sentence. Students have to decide which word / phrase you say and then number it. Use these sentences:

1 What did you *buy* at the shops?
2 You must arrive *on time*.
3 How do you *organise* your time?
4 He's very *punctual* in the morning.
5 Excuse me. I must go and talk to those *customers*.
6 You must file these papers in *alphabetical* order.
7 Put the times in *chronological* order.
8 Could you put all the files *in order*, please?
9 May I introduce my *colleague*, Mrs Jones?
10 What do you do in your *job*, exactly?
11 Could I speak to the *manager*, please?
12 I have got a very interesting *task* for you.

Feed back by saying each sentence again and getting the students to say the word or phrase from the box.

Exercise A

Students might find this more challenging than previous similar activities. If so, give them the possible pairs and ask them simply to give the explanations using the following language:

They are two ways ...
They are both ...
They both mean ...

Possible pairs:

manager	colleague
job	task
punctual	on time
organise	in order
customers	buy
alphabetical	chronological

Exercise B

1 Elicit two or three points, in any order, then set for pairwork.
2 Refer students to the blue table at the bottom of the page for self-checking. Make a copy of the outline of the blue table on the board while the students are working. Feed back by building up the list of points in the first column.

Answers
See Column 1 of the answers to Exercise D below.

Exercise C

Ask why you must do the first point. Elicit some ideas. Confirm good ones, even if they are not Gerald's reasons. Don't worry about the exact form of student contributions, as long as they can explain their ideas. Set for pairwork. Feed back, getting ideas in the second column of the table on the board.

Answers

The words in the second column will depend on the students.

Exercise D

1 Check that students understand the task. Play the recording. Students complete individually. Students discuss in pairs whether they have got the same stressed words. Feed back, getting some of the stressed words in the third column of the table on the board.
2 Check that students understand the task. Play the recording, twice if necessary. Elicit answers and ask some of the students to write their notes on the board for the rest of the class to compare. Check understanding of some of the key vocabulary.

Extra activity

Students cover the right-hand column. Say an action in the left-hand column and elicit the correct reason from the right-hand column. Make sure it is accurate. This could also be done in pairs.

Possible answers

You must ...	Our reasons	Gerald's reasons
go every day		rely
be punctual		expect you
respect your manager and your colleagues		work together
respect the customers		pay wages
do all the tasks that your manager gives you		boring tasks
complete all your tasks on time		need information
be responsible for the quality of your work		customer dissatisfied
keep your workplace tidy		rude / mess
organise your work files sensibly		ill / papers

Exercise E

Set the task and explain that different words will have to be used for *manager*, *colleague*, etc., perhaps *tutor* or *head of department* and *friends* or *fellow students*. Monitor while students are working in groups and give feedback.

Closure

Get a list of advice for students on the board.

Play the talk again (track 34 on CD1).

Lesson 1: Vocabulary

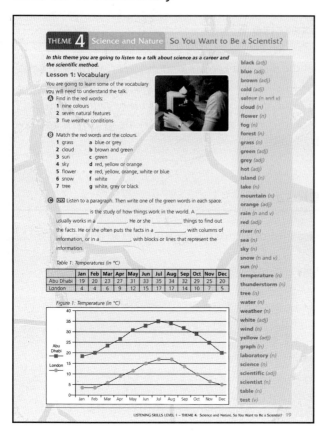

Introduction

Exploit the visual and use it to teach the word *scientist*. Write the question in the theme title on the board.

Exercise A

Set the task. Students complete individually. Elicit answers.

Revise the sounds of *g* by writing the words containing the letter *g* on the board and asking students to pronounce each word correctly.

Answers

1 nine colours: black, blue, brown, green, grey, orange, red, white, yellow

2 seven natural features: forest, island, lake, mountain, river, sea, sky

3 five weather conditions: (choose from) cloud, fog, rain, snow, sun, thunderstorm, wind

Exercise B

Set the task. Students complete individually. Elicit answers.

Say red words in isolation at random. Students point to the correct word on the list (see notes for Theme 1 Lesson 1).

Answers

1	grass	c	green
2	cloud	g	white, grey or black
3	sun	d	red, yellow or orange
4	sky	a	blue or grey
5	flower	e	red, yellow, orange, white or blue
6	snow	f	white
7	tree	b	brown and green

Exercise C

Say the green words. Set the task. Play the recording. Students complete individually, then compare answers. Play the recording again if necessary. Then write the correct answers on the board for students to self-correct.

Exploit the table and graph in order to teach all the necessary vocabulary: *facts, columns, blocks, lines, table, graph*.

Ask questions about the table, e.g.,

> *What's the average temperature in Abu Dhabi in October?*
> *What's the average temperature in London in January?*
> *How much hotter is Abu Dhabi than London in July?*

Point out that these are the *average* temperatures – therefore if it is 45°C in the middle of the day and 25°C at night, the average temperature is 45°C + 25°C = 70°C ÷ 2 = 35°C.

Answers

Science is the study of how things work in the world. A scientist usually works in a laboratory. He or she tests things to find out the facts. He or she often puts the facts in a table, with columns of information, or in a graph, with blocks or lines that represent the information.

Closure

1   Further exploit the table. Give a piece of data and get students to tell you what it represents, e.g.,

      Teacher: 19?
      Students: (Average) temperature in Abu Dhabi in January.

2   Further exploit the graph. Get students to cover the table and find the answers from the graph this time, e.g.,

      Teacher: What is the temperature in London in January?
      Students: (reading from the graph) 4.

Lesson 2: Listening

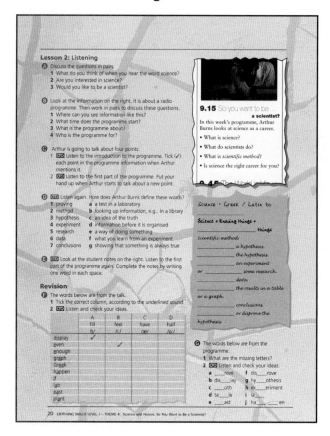

Introduction

Revise the green words from the previous lesson. Refer students to the visual to reinforce the idea of *scientist*. Elicit different kinds of scientist.

Language and culture note

There are words for the main branches of science that are nearly the same in Arabic (although there are other more common words in some cases):

chemistry – *keemia*
biology – *beeyooloogia*
physics – *fizia*

Exercise A

Set the task. Monitor. Ask some of the students to report back on their conversations.

If they all say they don't want to be a scientist, say perhaps this theme will change their minds!

Exercise B

Exploit the visual. Students read the extract. Students ask and answer the questions in pairs.
Elicit answers.

Answers
1   In a newspaper with TV and radio listings.
2   9.15.
3   Science as a career.
4   People who want to be scientists.

Exercise C

Set the task and play the recording. Elicit answers.

Answers
Topics will be as listed, and in the order listed.

Exercise D

Give students time to read everything through before you play the recording.

Students complete individually, then compare answers. Write the correct answers on the board for students to check. Go over any answers students had difficulty with.

1   g   showing that something is always true
2   e   a way of doing something
3   c   an idea of the truth
4   a   a test in a laboratory
5   b   looking up information, e.g., in a library
6   d   information before it is organised
7   f   what you learn from an experiment

Exercise E

This is a guided note-taking activity. Give students time to read the note extract. Set the task and play the recording.

Students complete individually then compare answers. Play the recording again if necessary.

Elicit the answers and write them on the board (NB: *just* the answers – see extra activity below), preferably using an OHT of the extract. Point out the word *test* here is used as a verb and that *draw* has a different meaning in this context.

Extra activity

Ask students to close their books. Use the list of correct answers on the board as prompts to elicit and consolidate the complete phrase, e.g.,

> Teacher: Make.
> Students: *Make a hypothesis.*

Answers

Science = Greek / Latin 'to <u>know</u>'
Science = knowing things + <u>proving</u> things
Scientific method:
<u>Make</u> a hypothesis.
<u>Test</u> the hypothesis
<u>Do</u> an experiment
or <u>do</u> some research.
<u>Collect</u> data.
<u>Display</u> the results in a table or a graph.
<u>Draw</u> conclusions.
<u>Prove</u> or disprove the hypothesis.

Exercise F

1 Students complete individually.
2 Play the recording. Students compare answers. Elicit answers and give extra pronunciation practice where necessary.

Answers

	A fill /ɪ/	B feel /iː/	C have /æ/	D half /ɑː/
di<u>s</u>play	✓			
<u>e</u>ven		✓		
<u>e</u>nough	✓			
gr<u>a</u>ph				✓
Gr<u>ee</u>k		✓		
h<u>a</u>ppen			✓	
<u>i</u>f	✓			
l<u>a</u>b			✓	
p<u>a</u>st				✓
pl<u>a</u>nt				✓

Exercise G

1 Students discuss in pairs.
2 Play the recording. Elicit answers. Give extra practice where necessary.

Answers

a prove
b display
c both
d table
e past
f disprove
g hypothesis
h experiment
i lab
j happen

Closure

Go back to Exercise D. Students have books closed. Give the definition and elicit the word.

Play the programme again (track 37 on CD1).

Lesson 3: Learning new skills

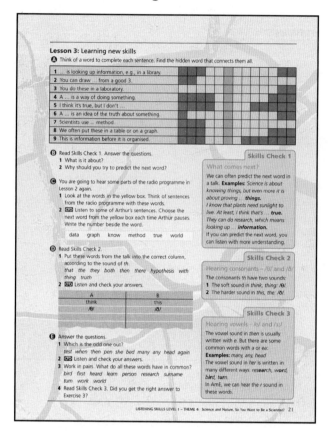

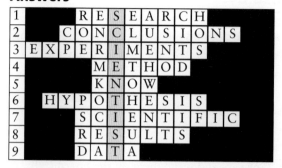

Introduction

Revise the talk given by Arthur Burns in Lesson 2. (If you prefer, play the recording again with the students following the tapescript on page 55 of their books.)

Exercise A

Tell students these are all words from Lesson 2 of this theme. If students find it difficult, supply the first letter of each word. Students do as much as they can individually, then continue with a partner. Elicit answers, checking for pronunciation and spelling.

Exercise B

Remind students how they predicted language, i.e., content in Theme 3 Lesson 4. This activity gives them more specific practice with this particular sub-skill.

EITHER follow the procedure for previous Skills Checks OR with students' books closed, write the example sentences on the board (or say them) without the final word in bold. Students try to predict / guess the final word.

Then students read the box and discuss the questions.

Answers
1   It's about predicting words.
2   It helps you to listen with understanding.

Exercise C

Check carefully that students understand the task.
1   Give plenty of time for students to remember what these words mean / how they were used in the radio programme but do not attempt to re-explain them. It is important that students find some kind of aural 'trace' in their own memories.
2   Play each sentence. Stop the recording when there is a pause. Students number the words in the yellow box. Feed back after each sentence then continue the recording for students to self-check. You may need to hold a sentence for a long time for students to consider and reject possibilities. Note that Arthur says each sentence again without

the pause so students get to hear the whole thing and hopefully can hear why it was that word.

Answers

Answers are on the recording and in the tapescript, page 56 of the Student's Book (page 103 here).

Methodology note

It may seem strange that students number the words, rather than simply saying them, but this is to give the weaker students more processing time to work out what comes next. Clearly, in real life you only have a split second – but if students do not believe it is possible, because they never prove to themselves that they can do it, they will never get up to real-world speed.

Extra activity

Read out other sentences from the talk for this theme or previous themes. Pause before the end of each sentence for students to predict the final word.

Exercise D

If you like, briefly revise pronunciation of words with *g* from the previous theme.
Say the words in Skills Check 2.
1 Set the task for individual completion.
2 Play the recording. Students compare answers. Practise saying some of the words.

Answers

A	B
think	this
/θ/	/ð/
thing	the
hypothesis	then
truth	they
both	there
	with
	that

Language and culture note

There are no blends in Arabic, so students will always have problems with the idea that two letters can make one sound. However, they will obviously have met this digraph with its two sounds many times before. In Arabic, both sounds exist but they are written as separate letters. In fact, there are three sounds in Arabic made at the same point of articulation, because they also have a pharyngealised version of the voiced consonant – it is best mimicked by saying the voiced sound with a slack jaw. This is so unusual that Arabs sometimes call themselves 'the people of *thaad*' and Arabic 'the language of *thaad*'.

When do we say the voiced and when do we say the unvoiced consonant? There are no teachable rules, except perhaps to say that the voiced consonant is more common in function words (*the*, *that*, *then*) and the unvoiced more common in content words (*thing*, *truth*, *hypothesis*).

Exercise E

1 Students discuss in pairs. Do not elicit the answer.
2 Play the recording. Elicit the answer.
3 Set a time limit of one minute to find the answer.
4 Read Skills Check 3 aloud, with the students following in their books. Ask students if they got the correct answer in Exercise 3.

Answers

1 / 2 *she* is the odd one out because it has a long /iː/.
3 They all have the sound /ɜː/.

Extra activity

Elicit more words with the sound in *her*.

Closure

Dictate some of the key words from this theme.

Lesson 4: Applying new skills

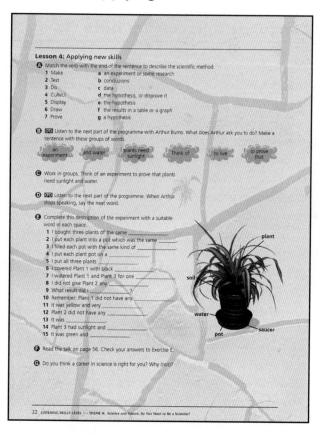

Lesson 4: Applying new skills

A Match the verb with the end of the sentence to describe the scientific method.
1 Make   a an experiment or some research
2 Test   b conclusions
3 Do   c data
4 Collect   d the hypothesis, or disprove it
5 Display   e the hypothesis
6 Draw   f the results in a table or a graph
7 Prove   g a hypothesis

B Listen to the next part of the programme with Arthur Burns. What does Arthur ask you to do? Make a sentence with these groups of words.

an experiment   and water   plants need sunlight   Think of   to live   to prove that

C Work in groups. Think of an experiment to prove that plants need sunlight and water.

D Listen to the next part of the programme. When Arthur stops speaking, say the next word.

E Complete this description of the experiment with a suitable word in each space.
1 I bought three plants of the same _____
2 I put each plant into a pot which was the same _____
3 I filled each pot with the same kind of _____
4 I put each plant pot on a _____
5 I put all three plants _____
6 I covered Plant 1 with black _____
7 I watered Plant 1 and Plant 3 for one _____
8 I did not give Plant 2 any _____
9 What result did I _____?
10 Remember: Plant 1 did not have any _____
11 It was yellow and very _____
12 Plant 2 did not have any _____
13 It was _____
14 Plant 3 had sunlight and _____
15 It was green and _____

plant
soil
water
pot   saucer

F Read the talk on page 56. Check your answers to Exercise E.

G Do you think a career in science is right for you? Why (not)?

22 LISTENING SKILLS LEVEL 1 – THEME 4: Science and Nature, So You Want to Be a Scientist?

Introduction

Revise the three previous lessons by doing a quiz, e.g.,
What does 'hypothesis' mean?
What's the difference between a table and a graph?
Where does the word 'science' come from?
What's the adjective from the word 'science'?

Exercise A

Set the task. Students complete individually then compare answers. Elicit answers.

Answers

1	Make	g	a hypothesis
2	Test	e	the hypothesis
3	Do	a	an experiment or some research
4	Collect	c	data
5	Display	f	the results in a table or a graph
6	Draw	b	conclusions
7	Prove	d	the hypothesis, or disprove it

Exercise B

Briefly remind students about the talks by the scientist, Arthur Burns, they have listened to. Set the task and play the recording. Students try to make the sentence. Then play the recording again. Elicit the answer.

Answer

Think of an experiment to prove that plants need sunlight and water to live.

Exercise C

Exploit the visual of the plant. If your students are not very scientific, they may need some clues, e.g.,
- you need three plants
- you need black plastic
- you need water

Do not elicit or confirm / correct at this stage.

Exercise D

Make sure students realise that they have to think of a suitable word this time – there is no list of words for them to number. Play each part up to the pause. As before, give weaker students a chance to think of something by preventing others shouting out. Then elicit ideas. Hold the learning tension for as long as necessary before allowing the recording to run on. Then say the whole sentence yourself without the pause. Move on to the next section plus pause.

Answers

Answers are on the recording and in the tapescript, page 56 of the Student's Book (page 104 here).

Exercise E

Students complete individually then compare answers. Do not elicit.

Exercise F

If you wish, play the recording while students are reading the talk. Remember – students may have answers that are correct but different from the ones given.

Give students the opportunity to ask about any other words in the talk they are unsure about the meaning of. You could also spend a few minutes focussing on the simple past tense verbs used throughout.

Answers

Answers depend on students, but here are possible sentences:

1 I bought three plants of the same <u>type</u>.
2 I put each plant into a pot which was the same <u>size</u>.
3 I filled each pot with the same kind of <u>soil</u>.
4 I put each plant pot on a <u>saucer</u>.
5 I put all three plants <u>outside</u>.
6 I covered Plant 1 with black <u>plastic</u>.
7 I watered Plant 1 and Plant 3 for one <u>week</u>.
8 I did not give Plant 2 any <u>water</u>.
9 What result did I <u>get</u>?
10 Remember: Plant 1 did not have any <u>sunlight</u>.
11 It was yellow and very <u>small</u>.
12 Plant 2 did not have any <u>water</u>.
13 It was <u>dead</u>.
14 Plant 3 had sunlight and <u>water</u>.
15 It was green and <u>healthy</u>.

Exercise G

This can be done as a class or paired activity.

Closure

Play the whole of the programme again. You will need to play track 37 on CD1 and tracks 3 and 4 on CD2.

You might like to end by mentioning the other key part of the scientific method – the idea of the fair test. What made the experiment in Exercise E a fair test?

Possible answers
The same plants.
He put them in pots the same size.
He used the same soil.
He put them all in the same place.

Lesson 1: Vocabulary

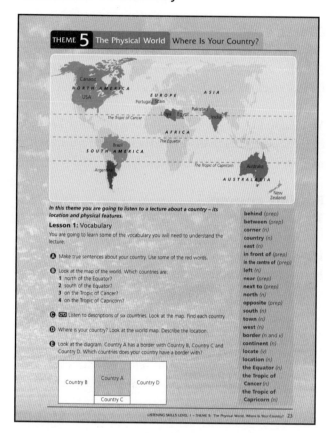

THEME 5 The Physical World Where Is Your Country?

*Strictly speaking, this is a little shorter but at this level it can be useful to stress the long sound at the end.

Exercise A

Elicit one or two sentences from students as examples. Write them on the board.

Students think of more sentences in pairs and write them down.

Ask some of the students to read out their sentences and correct them as necessary. Write the best / most interesting on the board.

Exercise B

Refer students to the world map. Check / teach the word *world*. Elicit the names of the continents and teach the word *continent*. Note that officially there is one more continent not marked – Antarctica. Ask students to find and point to *the Equator*, *the Tropic of Cancer* and *the Tropic of Capricorn*.

Set for pairwork. Feed back orally.

Answers

1 Canada, India, USA, Portugal, Spain, Libya, Egypt, Pakistan
2 Brazil, Argentina, Australia, New Zealand
3 India, Egypt, Libya
4 Brazil, Argentina, Australia

Introduction

Write the title of the theme on the board and elicit / teach the meaning of *physical*.

Ask students to put the red words into groups:
- directions
- prepositions of place
- physical features

Revise some of the sounds that the students have studied so far by asking students to find red words with these sounds:

/p/ *opposite*
/b/ *behind, between*
/ɪ/ *behind, between, in, river, mountain* (NOT the *i* in *behind* or *island*)
/iː/ *between, east, sea*, country* (NOT *near*)
/θ/ *north, south*
/ð/ *the* (in the centre of)
/e/ *centre, left, next, west*

Methodology note

Arguably it is not important in a listening course for students to be able to say the names of countries with an English pronunciation. However, you may feel this helps to understand the word when it is heard.

Language and culture note

In Arabic the word for Cancer also means *crab* and the word for Capricorn means *billy goat*. The same derivation exists for the words in English but we have lost the direct association between the name and the animal which existed in Latin. In both English and Arabic, the names are also used for star signs and constellations.

Many countries have almost the same name, although clearly a different pronunciation, in Arabic. Exceptions here are: the USA (strictly speaking *al walee'daat al moo'tahida* but widely called *al-amri'kiya*), Egypt (*misr*), India (*al-hind*).

Exercise C

Check students understand the task. Play the recording, pause after each sentence and replay if necessary. Students compare answers. Elicit answers.

Answers
1 Canada
2 India
3 Libya
4 Portugal
5 Australia
6 Brazil

Extra activities

1 Ask students to recall the sentences on the recording for each answer **accurately**, e.g.,
     Canada – *It is in North America. It is north of the USA.*
2 In pairs, one student describes another country on the map. The other tries to guess the name of the country. Then change round, e.g.,
     Student 1: It is in Africa. It is east of Libya.
     Student 2: It's Egypt.

3 Say some more large countries and get students to tell you which continent they are in. Obvious ones are China, Sudan, Russia, France. Students should also try to mark their approximate positions on the map. Give out atlases or display an OHT for them to check their own ideas.

Exercise D

Check / teach the meanings of the green words. Say each word. Elicit an answer from one of the students as an example. Students continue in pairs. Ask some of the students to say some of their sentences.

Exercise E

Ask students to draw a similar diagram and write a sentence about their country. Monitor and give feedback.

Closure

Build up a full paragraph about the students' countries on this pattern.
     (My country) is in (continent).
     It has borders with (countries).
     (Country A) is in the (direction). (etc.)

Lesson 2: Listening

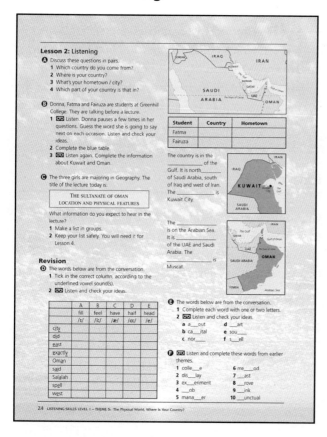

2   Give students time to read the table, then set the task. Students complete individually. Elicit answers.

3   Give students time to read the gapped text and study the maps. Students can write in any answers they might know already.

Play the recording. Students compare answers. Elicit answers.

Now, if you wish, play the recording with the students following the tapescript on page 56.

Note that there are two different ways to talk about the position of a country.

In Lesson 1, the position was given from 'my country' to neighbour. For example, describing the UAE, we could say:

Oman is in the south and east.

In this lesson, the position is given from neighbour to 'my country'. For example, describing the UAE, we could say:

The UAE is north and west of Oman.

Demonstrate this on a sketch map with arrows from, respectively, the country to neighbours and from neighbours to the country.

Introduction

Revise the green words from the previous lesson. Exploit the map at the top of the page using language from the previous lesson.

Exercise A

Set the task and divide the class into pairs. Monitor and give feedback.

Exercise B

1   Set the task. Students should be familiar with this type of prediction exercise. As detailed in previous lessons, you need to control the class carefully in order for the stronger (louder?) students not to dominate. Do this by either asking students to write the answer each time, or by only accepting answers from nominated students.

Answers

2 | Student | Country | Hometown |
| --- | --- | --- |
| Fatma | Kuwait | Al Khiran |
| Fairuza | Oman | Salalah |

3   Kuwait:
The country is in the <u>north</u> of the Gulf. It is north<u>east</u> of Saudi Arabia, south of Iraq and west of Iran. The <u>capital</u> is Kuwait City.
Oman:
The <u>country</u> is on the Arabian Sea. It is <u>southeast</u> of the UAE and Saudi Arabia. The <u>capital</u> is Muscat.

Language and culture note

There are three ways of referring to the body of water which stretches from Kuwait to the Straits of Hormuz. In American English, it is most commonly called the Persian Gulf. In British English, it is the Arabian Gulf or the Gulf. Allow your students to use whichever designation they are familiar with.

Exercise C

Students read the instructions and information. Check the meaning of *majoring*.

Elicit one or two examples and write them on the board. Then students continue in groups. Elicit answers. Check spelling and pronunciation where necessary.

Exercise D

1   Set the task. Point out that they will hear British English on this occasion. Students complete individually, then compare answers.
2   Play the recording. Elicit answers. Replay the recording if necessary.

Answers

	A fill /ɪ/	B feel /iː/	C have /æ/	D half /ɑː/	E head /e/
city	✓	✓			
did	✓				
east		✓			
exactly	✓	✓	✓		
Oman				✓	
said					✓
Salalah				✓	
spell					✓
west					✓

Exercise E

Follow the normal procedure.

Answers
1   about
2   capital
3   north
4   part
5   south
6   spell

Exercise F

Follow the normal procedure.

Answers
1   college
2   display
3   experiment
4   job
5   manager
6   method
7   past
8   prove
9   think
10 punctual

Closure

Ask students to close their books. Use the completed gapped texts from Exercise B3 as a dictation. This can be either a traditional dictation or follow one of the more 'communicative' ones.

Lesson 3: Learning new skills

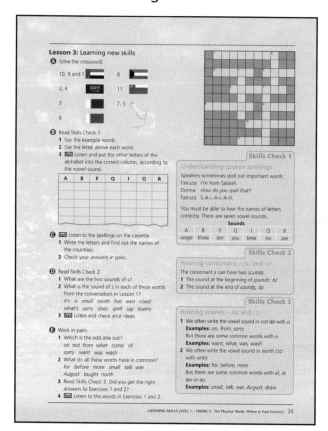

10, 9 and 1 United Arab Emirates

2, 4 Saudi Arabia

3 Qatar

6 Bahrain

8 Kuwait

11 Oman

7, 5 Arabian Gulf (see Language and culture note on page 47)

Introduction

Describe the location of a country. Students identify it. Use a local country or one from the theme so far.

Exercise A

Teach the word *flag*.

Set the task for individual completion. While the students are working on the crossword, write the alphabet on the board in preparation for the next exercise.

Elicit answers and check spelling. Ideally, feed back into an OHT of the crossword so students can try to spell out the words in each case. You can then take their spellings literally and put the wrong letters in as appropriate until other students correct. This will be good preparation for the next exercise.

Exercise B

1 After reading Skills Check 1, ask different students to read out an example word from the table at the bottom of the box. See if students can think of any other words with the same sound.

2 Say the letters and ask the students to repeat.

3 Do the exercise as suggested in the book, or let the students write the answers first then listen to check.

Answers

A B F Q I O R
H C L U Y
J D M W
K E N
  G S
  P X
  T Z**
  V
  Z*   *AmE   **BrE

Language and culture note

Notice that there is no one-to-one relationship between the letter name and its sound in English. Often the English letter name has the most common sound somewhere in it, at the beginning – e.g., Jay, Kay – or at the end – e.g., eM, eN. But at other times, the letter name has a less common sound – e.g., Cee, aR – and sometimes the letter sound is not even in the name – e.g., aitch, Y. All of this means there is a real learning task in associating the name of the letter with the sight of the letter. Long after students can correctly identify H or J, for example, they may not be able to instantly say the name.

In Arabic, by contrast, many letters have virtually the same name as the sound the letter makes – e.g., ba, ta, tha, ha, kha, ra, Ta, Za, etc. – so if you can spell the word, you can say the spelling out loud. Therefore the problems with 'spelling out' in English will surprise students and they will try to spell like in Primary School, e.g., *Arabic* = a - ra - a - ba - i - ka.

Exercise C

1   Set the task. Play the recording. Students complete individually. Do not elicit at this stage.
2   Students compare answers. Play the recording again if necessary. Write the correct answers on the board for students to check.

Extra activity

Give out pieces of paper with more lists of countries. Students work in pairs. One student has the list and spells out the country. The other student says the name of the country as soon as he/she can.

The students should identify the country at some stage of the spelling-out.

1   U-K
2   U-A-E
3   U-S-A
4   O-M-A-N
5   Q-A-T-A-R
6   K-U-W-A-I-T
7   B-A-H-R-A-I-N
8   Y-E-M-E-N
9   J-A-P-A-N
10 C-H-I-N-A
11 S-A-U-D-I A-R-A-B-I-A
12 G-U-L-F

The following letters are not used in the above and could be dictated separately: V, X, Z.

Exercise D

Read Skills Check 2 aloud, with the students following in their books. Check understanding.
1   Elicit answer – /s/ and /z/.
2   Students discuss in pairs. Do not elicit answers.
3   Play the recording, twice if necessary. Elicit answers.

Answers

/s/   it's   small   south   east   coast   what's   sorry   spell   say
/z/   is   has   does   towns

Language and culture note

The usual problem! In Arabic, both the sounds /s/ and /z/ exist – indeed, there is a third sound once again which is said with more force than /z/ and with a slack jaw. But there are separate letters for each sound. It is a complete mystery to an Arabic speaker why the letter *s*, for example, can be /s/ in one environment and /z/ in another. At this stage, do not try to explain about the effect of the environment – e.g., plural *s* has an unvoiced sound after an unvoiced consonant and a voiced sound after a vowel or voiced consonant. Just teach them to say the sound correctly in each case. Their ability at rote learning will do the rest.

Exercise E

1 and 2 Students discuss in pairs. Do not elicit answer.
3   After students have read the Skills Check, elicit
     answers.
4   Play the recording with the students looking at the
     words in their book.

Answers
1   come = not an /ɒ/ sound
2   They all have /ɔː/ (although the spelling is different).

Extra activity

With students' books closed, give a spelling test on
some of the words from Exercises D and E.

Lesson 4: Applying new skills

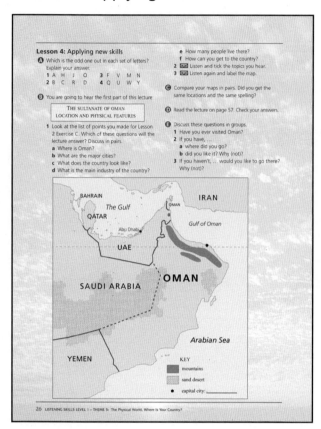

Introduction

Use Exercise A as an introduction to this lesson. This is a revision exercise. Students complete individually then compare answers. Elicit answers.

Answers

1   O hasn't got the /ei/ sound.
2   R hasn't got the /i:/ sound.
3   V hasn't got the /e/ sound.
4   Y hasn't got the /u:/ sound.

Exercise B

It would be helpful to have an OHT of the map for feedback.

1   Elicit the points listed in Lesson 2 Exercise C and write them on the board. Students read questions a–f. Compare the list of points on the board with the questions. Students add any extra topics to their lists. Students discuss in pairs which questions the recording will answer. Elicit some of their ideas but do not confirm or correct at this stage.

2   Play the recording. Students tick the topics they hear. Elicit answers. Students ask and answer the questions in pairs. (Note: Some of the questions are not answered on the recording. This should be predictable, since the topic is location and physical features – point this out.) It is not necessary for students to answer with full sentences; they only need to hear the key words.

3   Set the task. Play the recording, twice if necessary. Do not elicit answers at this stage.

Answers

a   north of the Equator – northwest UAE, northeast Gulf of Oman, west = Saudi Arabia, southeast Arabian Sea, southwest Yemen
b   not answered
c   stony desert, sandy desert, mountains
d   not answered
e   not answered
f   not answered

These are the topics from the book but students should have one more: size = 212,500 square kilometres.

Exercise C

Students can edit their maps during this stage.

Extra activity

Give out atlases or maps for students to check their work – either at this stage or after Exercise D below.

Exercise D

After reading, elicit answers on to an OHT on the board. Help with any other new vocabulary from the tapescript.

Some language points that could be followed up are:

location: *is located, is bordered by, to the west* v. *in the west*

area: *total area, three times the area of*

Methodology note

Remember – reading the tapescript of information that you have struggled to understand aurally is not *cheating*! At some point, you must be allowed to see the words which you have failed to understand in their spoken form. That is the last resort to be able to hear more effectively next time. Ideally, students should read and listen so their brains can begin to make the correct association.

Exercise E

Monitor and give feedback.

Closure

Get students to close their books and draw a sketch map of Oman – similar to the one at the bottom of Lesson 1. Working in groups or pairs, get them to fill in as much information as they can.

If they need help with the spelling of anything in English, dictate it. Compare the sketch maps at the end with a real map and declare a winner – give him or her the *Ibn Battuta prize for Geography*.

Play the lecture again (track 15 on CD2).

Language and culture note

Ibn Battuta was a great Arab traveller of the 14th century. He started on his travels, when he was 20 years old, in 1325. Originally he went on Hajj, or Pilgrimage to Mecca, as all good Muslims should do. But he continued travelling for nearly 30 years, covering about 75,000 miles and visiting the equivalent of 44 modern countries.

Lesson 1: Vocabulary

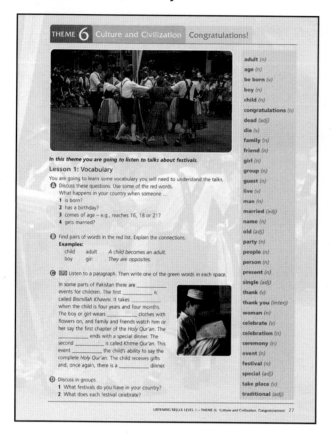

There are several words for *civilization* in Arabic. Perhaps the most useful in this context is *mada'nia*, from the root word for city – *me'dina* – because it contains the idea that civilization comes with city-living.

Introduction

Write the title of the theme on the board. Let students look up the words *culture* and *civilization* in their dictionary. Elicit the meaning / usage of *congratulations*.

Exploit the visual – elicit at least the idea that the people are wearing clothes that are special to their culture and doing a dance that is traditional – i.e., they do this dance on special occasions.

Language and culture note

The word *culture* in Arabic is in the name of the British Council in Arabic-speaking countries because it is called, in transliteration, *The British Cultural Council – 'majlis <u>tha'qafi</u> bara'Tania*.

Exercise A

Students discuss in pairs. With a weak class, you could even let them discuss the points in Arabic, then say some things in feedback with the red words.

Elicit some of their ideas.

Methodology note

If the students do all the skills books in this theme, this is a mild version of test-teach-test. By the end of this theme across all the skills, they should be capable of describing any or all of these events. At this stage, just allow them to say individual words in English.

Exercise B

Set the task and go over the examples. Students complete individually.

Students compare their ideas in pairs. Elicit answers.

Answers
Possible pairs:

child	adult	a child becomes an adult
boy	girl	opposites
live / be born	die	opposites
married	single	opposites
age	old	your age is how old you are
person	people	singular / plural
man	woman	opposites
present	party	you often give presents at parties

thank	present	you thank people for presents
guest	party	you have guests at a party

Exercise C

The text helps with the meanings of the green words. Read the green words aloud. Ask students if they know anything about *Bismillah Khawni*.

Set the task. Students listen and follow the text first **without** writing. Then let students write the words in the spaces.

Play the recording again. Elicit answers and check understanding of the green words further.

Answers

In some parts of Pakistan there are <u>traditional</u> events for children. The first <u>event</u> is called *Bismillah Khawni*. It takes <u>place</u> when the child is four years and four months. The boy or girl wears <u>special</u> clothes with flowers on, and family and friends watch him or her say the first chapter of the *Holy Qur'an*. The <u>celebration</u> ends with a special dinner. The second <u>event</u> is called *Khtme Qur'an*. This event <u>celebrates</u> the child's ability to say the complete *Holy Qur'an*. The child receives gifts and, once again, there is a <u>special</u> dinner.

Exercise D

Make this into a competition. Tell students they can have one point for every red word they use in their answers and two points for every green word. Appoint someone to keep score in each group. The rest of the group take it in turns to ask and answer the questions. At the end, ask the students with the highest scores to say some of their answers again for the whole class to hear.

Closure

Further exploit the text in C. Read up to a particular point and stop for students to provide the next word or phrase. Alternatively, read the text with mistakes for students to correct.

Lesson 2: Listening

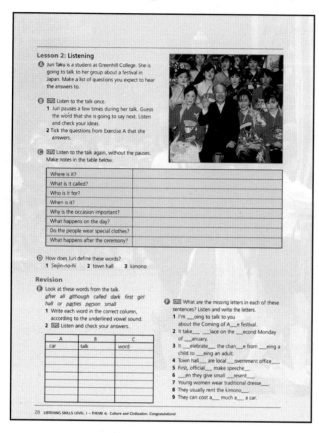

Lesson 2: Listening

A Juri Taku is a student at Greenhill College. She is going to talk to her group about a festival in Japan. Make a list of questions you expect to hear the answers to.

B Listen to the talk once.
1 Juri pauses a few times during her talk. Guess the word that she is going to say next. Listen and check your ideas.
2 Tick the questions from Exercise A that she answers.

C Listen to the talk again, without the pauses. Make notes in the table below.

Where is it?	
What is it called?	
Who is it for?	
When is it?	
Why is the occasion important?	
What happens on the day?	
Do the people wear special clothes?	
What happens after the ceremony?	

D How does Juri define these words?
1 *Seijin-no-hi*   2 town hall   3 kimono

Revision

E Look at these words from the talk.
after all although called dark first girl hall or parties person small
1 Write each word in the correct column, according to the underlined vowel sound.
2 Listen and check your answers.

A	B	C
car	talk	word

F What are the missing letters in each of these sentences? Listen and write the letters.
1 I'm ___oing to talk to you about the Coming of A___e festival.
2 It take___ ___lace on the ___econd Monday of ___anuary.
3 It ___elebrate___ the chan___e from ___eing a child to ___eing an adult.
4 Town hall___ are local ___overnment office___.
5 First, official___ make speeche___.
6 ___en they give small ___resent___.
7 Young women wear traditional dresse___.
8 They usually rent the kimono___.
9 They can cost a___ much a___ a car.

28 LISTENING SKILLS LEVEL 1 – THEME 6: Culture and Civilization, Congratulations!

Introduction

Revise the green words from the previous lesson.

Exercise A

Exploit the visual.

Set the task. Elicit one or two ideas for questions and write them on the board, e.g.,

What do you wear?
What do you celebrate?

Students continue in pairs. Elicit a few more questions and add them to the board.

Exercise B

1   Warning! Treat the first pause as a bit of fun! Set the task. Remind students why this is useful – it keeps you actively listening. Play the recording. Follow the normal procedure for this exercise.

2   Play the recording again so that students can tick the questions. Elicit the questions that were answered in the talk. Do not, however, elicit the answers to these questions as it may pre-empt Exercise C.

Exercise C

This activity practises the sub-skills of information transfer and using background knowledge.

Give students time to read the table and complete any answers they know already. Play the recording. Students complete individually, then compare answers.

Play the recording again. Elicit answers and write them on the board.

Answers
Model answers:

Where is it?	Japan
What is it called?	*Seijin-no-hi*
Who is it for?	All young people who become 20 years old in that year.
When is it?	The second Monday of January.
Why is it important?	Because in Japan after you are 20 you can vote (and smoke!).
What happens on the day?	There is a ceremony in local town halls. Government officials make speeches and give small presents to the new adults.
Do the people wear special clothes?	Yes, women wear kimonos. The kimonos are often rented as they can cost as much as a car. The men wear business suits, although a few wear dark kimonos.
What happens after the ceremony?	The young adults go to parties.

Exercise D

This activity practises intensive listening. See if students can remember; if not, play the recording again, pausing where appropriate.

Answers

1 the Coming of Age festival
2 offices of local government
3 traditional Japanese dress

Exercise E

1 Set the task. Students complete individually then compare answers.
2 Play the recording. Elicit answers.

Answers

A	B	C
car	*talk*	*word*
dark	hall	p<u>er</u>son
<u>a</u>fter	<u>a</u>lthough	girl
p<u>a</u>rties	called	first
	small	
	or	
	all	

Exercise F

Encourage students to complete as much as they can before you play the recording.

Play the recording. Then students compare answers. Elicit answers by asking students to read out the complete sentence each time.

Answers

1 I'm going to talk to you about the Coming of Age festival.
2 It takes place on the second Monday of January.
3 It celebrates the change from being a child to being an adult.

4 Town halls are local government offices.
5 First, officials make speeches.
6 Then they give small presents.
7 Young women wear traditional dresses.
8 They usually rent the kimonos.
9 They can cost as much as a car.

Closure

Play Bingo. Use these cards and the sentences below. The winner should shout after sentence 8 and should have Card 2 with the bottom line filled in

Card 1

festival	*speeches*	*event*
celebrates	*presents*	*suits*
traditional	*ceremony*	*adults*

Card 2

festival	*adults*	*ceremony*
presents	*suits*	*celebrates*
parties	*speeches*	*traditional*

Sentences
1 I'm going to talk to you today about a *festival* in Japan.
2 The festival *celebrates* coming of age.
3 There is a *ceremony* in a town hall.
4 First, government officials make *speeches*.
5 Then they give small *presents* to the new adults.
6 Young women wear *traditional* dresses called kimonos.
7 Young men wear business *suits* or, occasionally, dark kimonos.
8 Later, after the ceremony, there are special *parties*.
9 The boys and girls have become *adults*.

Play the talk again (track 18 on CD2).

Lesson 3: Learning new skills

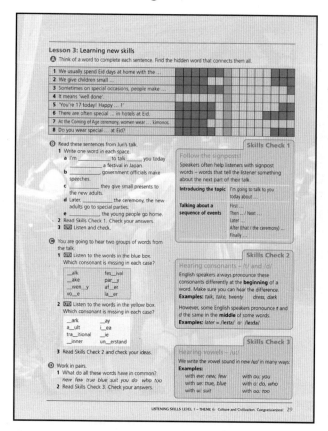

Introduction

Revise the festival of *Seijin-no-hi*; ask students if they can remember how this festival is celebrated.

Exercise A

Students complete individually then compare answers. If students find it difficult, give them the first letter of each answer.

When you elicit answers, get students to spell out the words to revise this skill. Ideally, feed back onto an OHT grid of the crossword.

Exercise B

1 Set the task. Students attempt it individually, but it does not matter if they cannot complete the exercise at this stage.
2 Elicit the everyday meaning of *signposts*. Read Skills Check 1 aloud, with the students following in their books. Students now check / complete Exercise 1.
3 Play the recording for checking; pause after each line if you wish. Students compare answers. Elicit answers.

Answers

a I'm <u>going</u> to talk <u>to</u> you today <u>about</u> a festival in Japan.
b <u>First</u>, government officials make speeches.
c <u>Then</u> they give small presents to the new adults.
d Later, <u>after</u> the ceremony, the new adults go to special parties.
e <u>Finally</u>, the young people go home.

Extra activity

Elicit then write on the board a brief list of local celebrations or events. Ask students to make three sentences about one of the events, using *First, Then, Finally.*

If you are going to do the other skills work for this theme, this is a preview. If not, it stands alone.

Exercise C

Give students plenty of time to look at the word in each box before playing the recording. Feed back, saying each of the sets of words again when you have confirmed the consonant so students clearly hear the difference. If you wish, point out that the place and manner of articulation are the same (don't say that, just show it!) but that one is unvoiced and the other is voiced.

Methodology note

Do not necessarily do listen and repeat for this kind of exercise. There is some evidence that saying a word correctly ensures that you can hear it correctly, but the main target of a listening course is, obviously, listening accurately, rather than producing accurately.

Exercise D

1 Students discuss in pairs. Do not elicit answers.
2 Read Skills Check 3 aloud, with students following in their books. Elicit the answer. Elicit more words with the same sound. Students make sentences using some of the words.

Answers
They all have the sound /uː/.

Closure

Say words from Exercise C at random and get students to say *t* or *d* – or even better /t/ or /d/. Add more examples. Make sure you include minimal pairs including ones with the /uː/ sound, i.e.,

    tie / die
    try / dry
    had / hat
    two / do
    true / drew

Lesson 4: Applying new skills

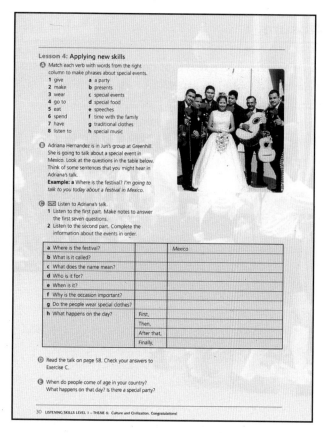

4	go to	a	a party
5	eat	d	special food
6	spend	f	time with the family
7	have	c	special events
8	listen to	h	special music

Exercise B

Students read the information. Exploit the visual and use it to predict some of the sentences from Adriana's talk. Use the actual questions in the table to predict more language.

Exercise C

1 Check students understand the task. Play the recording for part one. Students complete individually. Play part one again. Students compare answers.

2 Check students understand the task. Play the recording for part two. Students complete individually. Play part two again. Students compare answers.

Write the questions on the board in preparation for the feedback.

Introduction

Give a reverse dictation, i.e., tell students to pick out some key words from this unit and spell them to you; you write them on the board – exactly as they spell them!

Exercise A

Set the task. Students complete individually then compare answers. Elicit answers.

Now ask students to give you a full sentence using each phrase. The verb form can be changed if necessary, e.g., *Last week I gave a present to my sister for her wedding. I have never made a speech.*

Answers

1	give	b	presents
2	make	e	speeches
3	wear	g	traditional clothes

Exercise D

After students have finished reading the talk and checking their work, elicit answers. Build up the table on the board.

Answers
Model answer:

a	Where is the festival?	Mexico
b	What is it called?	Quinceanera
c	What does the name mean?	Fifteen years
d	Who is it for?	Girls
e	When is it?	When a girl becomes 15 years old.

f	Why is the occasion important?	It is a coming of age celebration. In the past in Mexico, parents expected a daughter to get married after she was 15.
g	Do the people wear special clothes?	The girl usually wears a long pink or white dress.
h	What happens on the day?	First, the girl's family and friends go to a ceremony in a church. Then, there are speeches, and fourteen couples walk with the birthday girl. After that, the girl gives a small doll to her younger sister. Finally, there is a party in a local hall, or at the home of the girl's parents.

Exercise E and Closure

Elicit ideas from the class and write notes on the board. Divide students into pairs. Encourage them to use *first, finally*, etc., in their discussion.

Finally, students could write a few sentences for consolidation.

Play the whole of the talk again. You will need to play tracks 25 and 26 on CD2.

Extra activities

1   Students ask and answer the questions from the table. Erase parts of the questions, leaving prompts. Students make questions, books closed.
2   Students tell each other what happens on the day using *first, then, after that, finally*. If you like, prompts can be written on the board for this exercise, too.

Lesson 1: Vocabulary

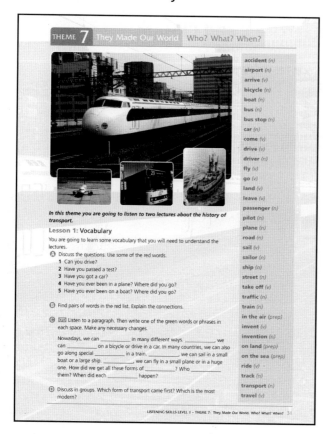

Remember – the key focus of this module is listening. As far as possible, let students get information from the listening text, rather than from written forms.

Introduction

Get students to identify the forms of transport in the picture.

Exercise A

Put students in groups to discuss the questions. Feed back with the whole class.

Exercise B

Students should be familiar with this activity by now. Give a few examples and set for pairwork. Feed back.

Answers

Example pairs:
arrive – leave
come – go
drive – car
fly – plane

Exercise C

Ask students to try to pronounce the green words. Elicit a few ideas in each case, then model the correct pronunciation. It is not important to drill at this point, since the focus here is on listening and associating the written word with the sound.

Note: Students should by now be able to predict the /sh/ in *invention* and the short /æ/ in *track*, *travel*, *transport*. The pronunciation of *ui* in *cruise* is the sound in *juice*, *suit*, *fruit*, which the students should know, but they might associate the letters with the sound in *build*.

Don't deal with the meaning of any new words at this stage.

Play the recording, several times if necessary. Feed back. After the words have been correctly identified, get students to close their books. Read the text again, pausing before the key words. Students complete. Then go through again, making mistakes in key words, or putting in the word *banana* or *elephant* instead of the target words.

Language and culture note

As English is not a phonemic language, it is never possible to be sure of the pronunciation of a new word. However, unless you can associate the sight of a word with its sound, it is unlikely that you will be able to identify it in the stream of speech.

Answers

Nowadays, we can <u>travel</u> in many different ways. <u>On land</u>, we can <u>ride</u> on a bicycle or drive in a car. In many countries, we can also go along special <u>tracks</u> in a train. <u>On the sea</u>, we can sail in a small boat or a large ship. <u>In the air</u>, we can fly in a small plane or in a huge one. How did we get all these forms of <u>transport</u>? Who <u>invented</u> them? When did each <u>invention</u> happen?

Exercise D

Set up the discussion. Don't feed back on this. It is an activity to raise interest in the next lesson. Tell students they will find out the answers next time.

Closure

Say a syllable from one of the target words in this lesson. Ask students to think of a word with that sound.

Examples:

/iː/	*leave, street*
/aɪ/	*arrive, drive, driver, fly, pilot, ride*
/ɑ/	*accident, land, passenger, track, traffic, transport, travel*
/eɪ/	*sail, sailor, take (off), train*

Lesson 2: Listening

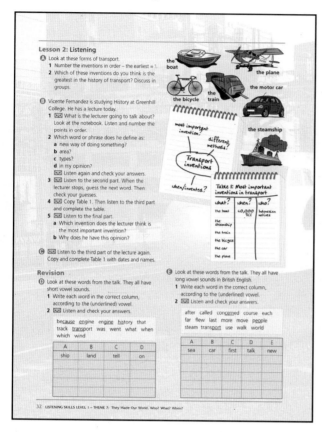

Remember – This is the revision lesson in the module. Take any opportunity to revise the following areas:
- understanding spoken definitions;
- understanding spoken times;
- identifying important words, predicting content;
- predicting next word;
- understanding spoken spelling;
- understanding signpost language.

Introduction

Do some revision of the sounds of key words.
Remind students of the question at the end of Lesson 1.

Exercise A

Set for pairwork or groupwork completion. Do not feed back on this – it is the content of the listening text in this lesson.

Exercise B

1 Refer students to the notebook. Give them time to think about a logical order for the points. Play the recording. Feed back.

2 Give students time to read the definitions for this activity. Explain that *area* in this case means *area of study*, not the size of a country, for example. Play the recording. Pause if necessary at key points. Feed back.

3 Follow usual procedure for this activity. Don't let strong students shout out until everybody has had a chance to think. After you confirm the correct answer, say that part of the talk again.

4 Give students time to copy the table – or give out a handout version of the table – see below. Play the recording; play again, pausing if necessary. Feed back, ideally onto an OHT. Ask students if they guessed the correct order in Exercise A.

5 Set the questions, then play the recording. Feed back with the whole class. Elicit a few ideas before confirming or correcting.

Answers

1 Order:
   a What are the different methods of transport?
   b When were they invented?
   c Which is the most important invention?

2 a invention
   b field
   c method
   d as far as I'm concerned

4 Model notes:

1	*the boat*	40,000 BCE	*Indonesian natives*
2	*the steamship*	1775	J.C. Perier
3	*the train*	1829	Stephenson
4	*the bicycle*	1839	Macmillan
5	*the car*	1888	Benz
6	*the plane*	1903	The Wright Brothers

5 He thinks the plane is the most important invention because it makes travel between countries easier, and this leads to greater understanding between people.

Exercise C

Refer students to the table and copy the initial table on to the board. Play the main part of the lecture again. Suggest that students make notes while they are listening. Play the lecture again if necessary. Feed back by completing the table on the board.

what?	when?	who?
the boat	40,000 BCE	*Indonesian natives*
the steamship	1775	J.C. Perier
the train	1830	Stephenson
the bicycle	1839	Macmillan
the car	1888	Benz
the plane	1903	The Wright Brothers

Language and culture note

BCE in the table means *Before the Common Era.* This is sometimes used in multicultural situations nowadays to avoid saying *Before Christ.* Although Muslims believe in Jesus, they see him as a prophet not as Christ, i.e., the son of God.

Exercises D and E

Follow the usual procedures for these revision activities.

Answers
D

A	B	C	D
ship	land	tell	on
which	track	when	was
wind	transport	went	what
history	that	engine	because
engine			

E

A	B	C	D	E
sea	car	first	talk	new
steam	after	world	course	flew
each	last	concerned	transport	move
people	far		called	use
			more	
			walk	

Closure

Get students to close their books and try to remember information from the lecture. Focus on the content rather than the form of their answers on this occasion.

Table 1: Most important inventions in transport

what?	when?	who?
the boat	40,000 BCE	*Indonesian natives*
the steamship		
the train		
the bicycle		
the car		
the plane		

Play the whole lecture again. You will need to play tracks 28 and 30–32 on CD2.

Lesson 3: Learning new skills

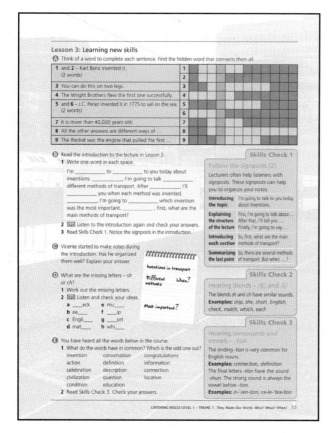

Exercise B

The aim of this activity is to use the students' aural memory to reconstruct part of the lecture in Lesson 2. Do not feed back before the students have had a chance to listen to the recording and correct their own work. Work on the content of the Skills Check by starting one of the sentences and getting students to tell you what you are doing, e.g.,

I'm going to …	You are introducing the topic.
First, I'm going to …	You are explaining the structure of the lecture.
Finally, I'm going to …	You are explaining the structure of the lecture.
So, first, …	You are introducing the first section.
So, there are several…	You are summarising the last point.

Introduction

Give students dates of inventions and names of inventors from the previous lesson and see if they can remember which invention they relate to, e.g.,
40,000 BCE – when the boat was invented
Indonesian natives – they invented the boat.

Exercise A

Set the puzzle as before. Feed back by getting students to produce the answers and identify the hidden word.

Answers

I'm going to talk to you today about inventions. First, I'm going to talk about different methods of transport. After that, I'll tell you when each method was invented. Finally, I'm going to say which invention was the most important. So, first, what are the main methods of transport?

Exercise C

It is very important that students should be able to predict the organisation of content in a lecture from the introductory words of the lecturer. Point out how helpful this is to understand the content when you hear it. Set the question, perhaps as a whole class.

Answers
Yes, because his notes follow the information in the introduction.

Exercise D

Give students time to try to identify words that contain the /ʃ/ or /tʃ/ sounds. Play the recording for students to check answers. Feed back, but do not drill pronunciation – remember: listening not speaking.

Answers
a   check
b   each
c   English
d   match
e   much
f   ship
g   short
h   which

Language and culture note

The two phonemes /ʃ/ and /tʃ/ exist in Arabic, so students should have little difficulty in discriminating them. They will not necessarily expect to hear the sounds in certain contexts, however, e.g., /tʃ/ in -ture and /ʃ/ in -tion.

Exercise E

Give students time to read all the words and identify commonality and the odd one out. Elicit ideas, but do not confirm or correct. Then give students time to read Skills Check 3.

Answers
They all end in -tion, but question is the odd one out because it does not have the shun pronunciation.

Closure

Spell some of the new words from the module for students to write down.

Lesson 4: Applying new skills

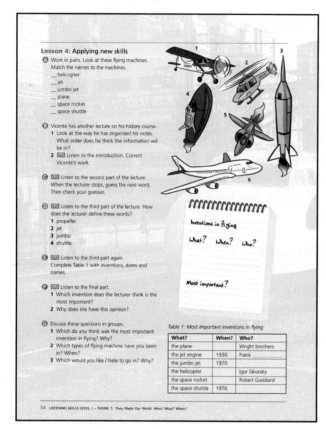

Introduction

Remind students of the signpost language from the last lesson. Build up the table from Skills Check 1 (Lesson 3) on the board.

Exercise A

Set as pairwork. Feed back.

Answers
1 plane
2 helicopter
3 space rocket
4 space shuttle
5 jet plane
6 jumbo jet

Language and culture note

Arabic has meaningful roots and uses these roots much more extensively than we do in English. For example, you could say in Arabic the equivalent of:

The flyer flew the flying machine on a flight from the flying place.

It is therefore very difficult for Arabic speakers to understand that words connected with the same activity do not share any formal spelling relationship. Compare:

The pilot flew the plane on a flight from the airport.

In this particular case, the root – *tyr* = fly – exists in the Arabic words for plane and jet, and in the phrase for helicopter.

Exercise B

Remind students of the importance of predicting the order of information in a lecture from the introduction. Refer students to Vicente's notes.
1 Ask the question. Elicit answers, then confirm / correct.
2 Play the introduction. Give students time to correct the notes. Elicit and confirm / correct.

Answers
Vicente's notes are well set out and do not need correcting.

Exercise C

Follow the usual procedure for this activity.

Exercise D

Give students time to read and think about the pronunciation of the words. Put the table up on the board while students are working. Play the recording. Feed back.

Answers

1   propeller = pieces of wood that turn to pull the plane through the air
2   jet = very fast stream of air
3   jumbo = very big
4   shuttle = something that goes to a place and comes back

Exercise E

Refer students to the table and ask them if they know any of the answers. Elicit some ideas / guesses.

Play the recording. Students complete the table. Feed back by building up the table on the board.

Answers

The complete table:

Table 1: Most important inventions in flying

What?	When?	Who?
the plane	1903	Wright brothers
the jet engine	1930	Frank Whittle
the jumbo jet	1970	Boeing
the helicopter	1910	Igor Sikorsky
the space rocket	1926	Robert Goddard
the space shuttle	1976	NASA

Exercise F

Ask the students what the lecturer is going to talk about at the end. Elicit answers. Set the questions. Play the recording. Elicit ideas. Play the final part again if necessary.

Answers

She thinks the shuttle is the most important; it has helped us reach out into space, to see how small the Earth is and to understand that it needs looking after.

Exercise G and Closure

Use this activity as the closure.

Play the whole lecture again. You will need to play tracks 38–40 and 42 on CD2.

Lesson 1: Vocabulary

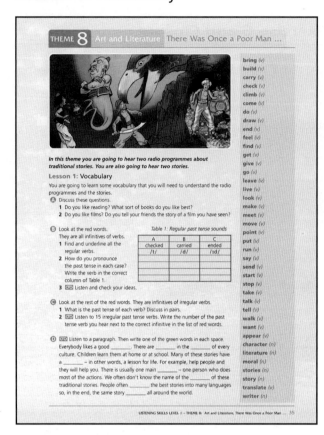

Remember that this is a listening module. Take every opportunity to give information in speech and with the recording. It is not necessary to drill or teach the spelling of any of the vocabulary, as the focus is on understanding it in speech, not on speaking it or writing.

These are the skills that students have learnt to date (most are revised in Lesson 2):
- understanding spoken definitions;
- following instructions;
- identifying names;
- understanding spoken times;
- identifying important words;
- predicting content;
- predicting next word;
- understanding spoken spelling;
- understanding signpost language;
- identifying dates.

Introduction and Exercise A

Use Exercise A as an introduction to this lesson. Hold a general discussion.

Exercise B

Follow the procedure set for the first part. Then build up the table on the board, indicating the three sounds with the example words.

Play the recording. Feed back onto the board. Get students to identify when the /ɪd/ sound will appear, i.e., when the infinitive ends in *t* or *d*.

Answers
Table 1: Regular past tense sounds

A *checked* /t/	B *carried* /d/	C *ended* /ɪd/
looked	climbed	pointed
stopped	moved	waited
talked	lived	started
walked		wanted

Methodology note

There are a large number of verbs for revision in this module. It is essential that students can recognise in speech the past tense of a large range of verbs – regular and irregular – if they are to be able to follow spoken stories.

Note that very few regular past tense endings have an audible sign in the stream of speech. Only where the infinitive ends in *t* or *d* will students hear a 'pastness' marker. The first teaching point here is therefore to show that they should not listen for /ɪd/ with words like *stop*. The past tense endings of other regular verbs are very difficult to hear. Indeed, they are not audible at all when the past tense verb is followed by most consonants.

Examples:

He carried the bag.

She checked to see ...

They stopped by the river.

It is not useful to spend a long time getting students to try to hear these sounds in context, therefore. The contrary point is the useful one to teach: i.e., because you *can't* hear the regular past tense endings /t/ and /d/, you should not try to hear them. Listen for other indications of 'pastness'.

Exercise C

Make sure students understand the difference between a regular verb – one that has an '*ed*' past tense – and an irregular verb. Point out that there are patterns in irregular past tenses but generally it is best just to learn the word and be able to identify it in speech.

1 Give students plenty of time to try to remember the past tense, but don't drill the words – remember, this is listening.

2 Play the recording. Pause after each word, if necessary, to give students time to link it.

Answers

1	said – say	9	got – get
2	came – come	10	went – go
3	found – find	11	put – put
4	left – leave	12	sent – send
5	gave – give	13	ran – run
6	told – tell	14	brought – bring
7	took – take	15	built – build
8	met – meet		

Language and culture note

Arabic is based on trilaterals – three consonants that make different parts of speech and associated words through the addition of short and long vowels and affixes. These trilaterals are basically the past tense of verbs, so one could say that Arabs store meaning through the simple past and then link other forms – simple present, nouns – to that. In English, however, it is likely that we store meaning with the infinitive / unmarked present simple and link to that.

Methodology note

It is essential that students should link a past tense instantly with its infinitive, as the infinitive / unmarked present tense is likely to be the way the word is stored in their memory. Work on this instant identification throughout this module.

Exercise D

Refer students to the green words. Say the words if you wish, but do not deal with the meaning.

Play the recording. Give students time to identify the words. Feed back by reading the text and getting students to tell you the missing word in each case. Deal with any problems with meaning.

Methodology note

It is very important for students to have practice in identifying a new word in context. Unless you can do this, you cannot seek help on its meaning.

Answers

Everybody likes a good <u>story</u>. There are <u>stories</u> in the <u>literature</u> of every culture. Children learn them at home or at school. Many of these stories have a <u>moral</u> – in other words, a lesson for life. For example, help people and they will help you. There is usually one main <u>character</u> – one person who does most of the actions. We often don't know the name of the <u>writer</u> of these traditional stories. People often <u>translate</u> the best stories into many languages so, in the end, the same story <u>appears</u> all around the world.

Closure

Return to identifying infinitives from the past simple. Play a game. Put students into teams. You say a past tense. Teams shout out the correct infinitive to get a point.

Lesson 2: Listening

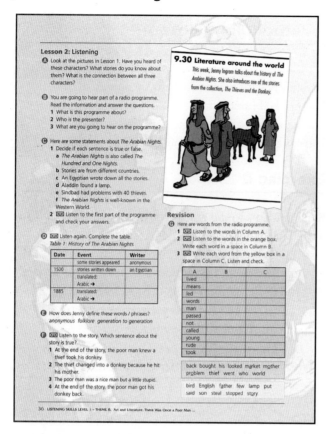

Introduction

Quickly check the identification of past simple verbs.

Exercise A

Exploit the visuals. The more you can elicit of the stories behind these pictures, the better you will have built the schemata for the listening in this lesson. Make sure you teach at least the following:

> Aladdin – lamp;
> Sindbad – Roc (a bird that is not real);
> Ali Baba – if possible, elicit 'thieves' but don't push it if they don't know the story.

Elicit (if possible) that the connection between the three characters is *The Arabian Nights*. If students don't know this, leave this point to Exercise B.

Exercise B

Refer students to the text from a listings magazine. Ask students where they can see a text like this (a newspaper or magazine with information about TV and radio programmes).

Set for pairwork. Feed back with the whole class. If students did not get the connection between the characters in A, explain it now.

Answers

1 It's about the history of *The Arabian Nights* (which contains the three characters in A).
2 Jenny Ingram.
3 Something about history, then a story.

Methodology note

This is a listening lesson but it is essential that the correct schemata are activated or listening will be difficult or impossible. We rarely listen to anything without preparing ourselves first, by reading about it or thinking about it. The listings extract here is a device to get the schemata activated.

Exercise C

Work through the statements, perhaps as a whole class. Play the recording, pausing to let students discuss each point.

Answers

a False – *The Thousand and One Nights*
b True
c True – point out that he wrote them down, but they existed long before.
d True
e False – Sindbad met the Roc; Ali Baba met the Forty Thieves.
f True

Methodology note

Listening to confirm predictions is a powerful skill, and far better than simply listening for information in which you have no personal stake.

Exercise D

Refer students to the table. Play the first part of the programme again. Feed back by building up the table on the board.

Answers

Date	Event	Writer
800	some stories appeared	anonymous
1500	stories written down	an Egyptian
1717	translated: Arabic → French	Galland
1885	translated: Arabic → English	Burton

Exercise E

Students have learnt to pick out definitions. Play the first part again if necessary.

Answers

anonymous = nobody knows who wrote the stories
folklore = the traditional stories from a culture
generation to generation = father to son, mother to daughter

Exercise F

Play the story once. See if students can identify the correct sentence. If not, play the recording again. Allow students to see the transcript at some point.

Answer

3   The poor man was a nice man but a little stupid.

Extra activity

You can do a lot more listening work with the story, as follows:

1   Play the recording and pause for students to give the next word.
2   Tell the story and make mistakes – funny mistakes if possible. Students correct.

Exercise G

This activity covers all the vowel sounds so far – short and long. They are in pairs, e.g., /ɪ/ then /iː/, except for the last three. Copy the table on to the board or use an OHT.
1   Play the recording of Column A. Students can repeat, but don't drill.
2   Play the recording of Column B. Students copy words into the correct row. Feed back on this before moving on to 3.
3   Students try to complete Column C. Play the recording of Column C. Feed back onto the board.

Answers

A	B	C
lived	his	English
means	thief	steal
led	went	said
words	world	bird
man	back	lamp
passed	market	father
not	problem	stopped
called	bought	story
young	mother	son
rude	who	few
took	looked	put

Closure

Many stories in *The Arabian Nights* have a moral – a lesson for life. Ask the students: Is there a moral to this story? Perhaps it is telling us, 'Don't believe everything you hear.' Or perhaps there is no moral – it is just a funny story.

Play the whole programme again. You will need to play tracks 2 and 4 on CD3.

Lesson 3: Learning new skills

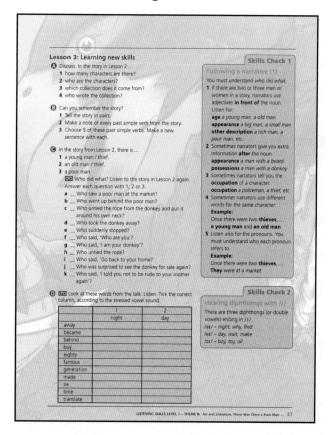

Introduction

Ask students how much they can remember about *The Arabian Nights*. See if they can remember some or all of the information from the table in Lesson 2.

Exercise A

Whole-class discussion.

Answers
1 three
2 A young thief, an old thief and a poor man.
3 *The Arabian Nights / A Thousand and One Nights.*
4 We don't know – the stories are anonymous.

Exercise B

You can spend a lot of time on Skills Check 1, getting students to reconstruct it in part or whole.

Follow the procedure as written. Go round the class eliciting sentences for Exercise B3.

Feed back going round the class eliciting sentences.

Exercise C

First get the students to write 1 next to 'a young man / thief', 2 next to 'an old man / thief', and 3 next to 'a poor man'. Make sure they understand their key for answering the question. Then follow the procedure as written.

Feed back orally – get students to substitute the correct person / people in their answer, e.g.,

    Teacher: Who saw a poor man at the market?
    Students: The (two) thieves saw …

Answers
a 1 and 2
b 1
c 1
d 2
e 1
f 3
g 1
h 3
i 3
j 3
k 3

Exercise D

Make sure students understand that the two words at the top are examples of two of the diphthongs in Skills Check 2. Model the sounds – *night* and *day* – to help students identify the appropriate sound. Note that the stressed vowel is not marked, so the students must identify this before completing the task.

Answers

	1 night	2 day
away		✓
became		✓
behind	✓	
buy	✓	
eighty		✓
famous		✓
generation		✓
made		✓
tie	✓	
time	✓	
translate		✓

Closure

Get students to suggest some more words with the two diphthongs from Exercise D (or all three from Skills Check 2).

Lesson 4: Applying new skills

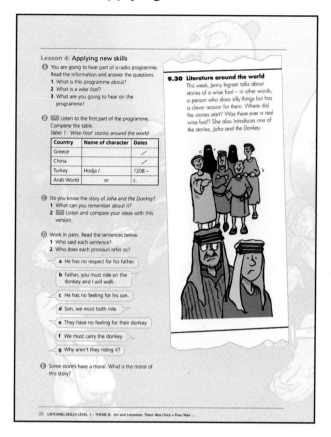

Introduction

Elicit what the students remember of the story in Lesson 2.

Exercise A

Students read the listings extract, then discuss the questions as a class.

Answers

1   Stories of a wise fool.
2   A person who does silly things but has a clever reason for them.
3   The history of the stories and one of the stories.

Exercise B

Deal with this section as in Lesson 2, Exercise D.

Answers

Country	Name of character	Dates
Greece	Chotzas	/
China	Afandi	/
Turkey	Hodja / Nasreddin	1208–1284
Arab World	Joha or Goha	c750

Exercise C

It is likely that this story is known to the students – at least, to some of them. If it is not known or recognised for some reason, give a little background to help students to understand the story they will hear. Perhaps draw a map on the board to show that Joha and his son are going from his village to a market town, passing through a couple of villages on the way.

Exercise D

Point out that these are sentences from the story. Identify the first one or two together and make sure that students can correctly identify the referents of the pronouns. Feed back.

Answers

a   an old man – *he* = Joha's son
b   Joha's son – *you* = Joha, *I* = his son
c   a young boy – *he / his* = Joha
d   Joha – *we* = Joha and his son
e   a man with a donkey – *they / their* = Joha and his son
f   Joha = *we* – Joha and his son
g   all the people at the market – *they* = Joha and his son

Exercise E and Closure

General discussion. Possibly the moral is: 'You can't make everybody happy.'

Play the whole programme again. You will need to play tracks 10 and 11 on CD3.

Lesson 1: Vocabulary

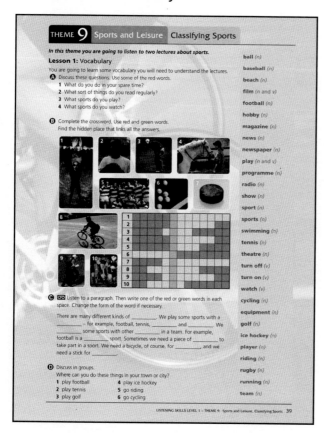

- understanding spoken definitions;
- understanding spoken times;
- identifying important words;
- predicting content;
- predicting next word;
- understanding spoken spelling;
- understanding signpost language;
- following a narrative;
- following instructions;
- identifying names;
- identifying dates.

Introduction

Explain that the module is about sports and leisure. Write the two words on the board and say some of the red words. Ask students to say whether the word is from the category sports or from leisure. (There are obvious overlaps, but the only point here is the broad distinction.) A subsidiary aim here is getting the students used to hearing these words, since this is a listening lesson.

Exercise A

Set for group discussion. Feed back with the whole class. Take the opportunity to give as much listening practice as possible by asking questions about the red words, e.g., *What about football?* etc.

Exercise B

Set for pairwork completion. Feed back, ideally on to an OHT grid. Get students to cover the answers and say the words at random. Students must say the correct clue number.

These are the phonemes that have been covered in the course to date. Take every opportunity to revise these phonemes, in addition to the set-piece revision in Lesson 2:

/p/ and /b/;

/g/ and /dʒ/;

/tʃ/ and /dʒ/;

/s/ and /z/;

/t/ and /d/;

/ʃ/ , /tʃ/ , /θ/ and /ð/;

/ɪ/ and /iː/;

/æ/ and /ɑː/;

/e/ and /ə/;

/ɒ/ and /ɔː/;

/uː/;

/eɪ/ /aɪ/ and /ɔɪ/.

These are the listening skills that have been covered in the course to date. Take every opportunity to revise these skills, in addition to the set-piece revision of some points in Lesson 2:

Answers

1				S	W	I	M	M	I	N	G
2				P	L	A	Y	E	R		
3			G	O	L	F					
4				R	I	D	I	N	G		
5				T	E	A	M				
6	T	E	N	N	I	S					
7	I	C	E	H	O	C	K	E	Y		
8			C	Y	C	L	I	N	G		
9				R	U	N	N	I	N	G	
10		R	U	G	B	Y					

Exercise C

Follow the normal procedure.

Answers

There are many different kinds of <u>sport</u>. We play some sports with a <u>ball</u> – for example, football, tennis, <u>rugby</u> and <u>golf</u>. We <u>play</u> some sports with other <u>players</u> in a team. For example, football is a <u>team</u> sport. Sometimes we need a piece of <u>equipment</u> to take part in a sport. We need a bicycle, of course, for <u>cycling</u>, and we need a stick for <u>ice hockey</u>.

Exercise D

Set for group discussion. Monitor. Feed back.

Closure

Say 10 red and green words. Ask students to number them in the order you say them. If you wish, repeat the activity with a different 10 words, but this time in context. These activities practise the vital listening skills of hearing words in isolation and in the stream of speech.

Lesson 2: Listening

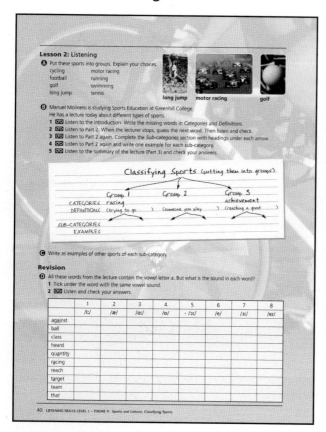

Introduction

Elicit the names of as many sports as you can. Perhaps try the Alphabet of Sports game, i.e., *Can you think of a sport beginning with …?*

A   athletics, archery
B   baseball, basketball, badminton
C   cricket
D   darts
E   equestrianism
F   football, fencing
G   golf
H   hockey
J   judo (etc.)

It doesn't matter if the students can't think of a sport for every letter. Just move on to the next letter, or give letters at random if you know there is a well-known sport for those letters.

Exercise A

Set for pairwork. If the students are struggling, suggest the two possible groupings in the answer and set the activity for them to fill in the sports. Feed back. Make sure you use the target words a lot so that the students get used to hearing them.

Answers

The answers really depend on the students, but possible ways of grouping the sports are as follows:

ball sports	others
football	cycling
golf	long jump
tennis	motor racing
	running
	swimming

sports with special equipment	others
cycling	football
motor racing	long jump
golf	running
tennis	swimming

Exercises B and C

Follow the usual procedure for listening activities.

Answers

Classifying Sports (putting them into groups)

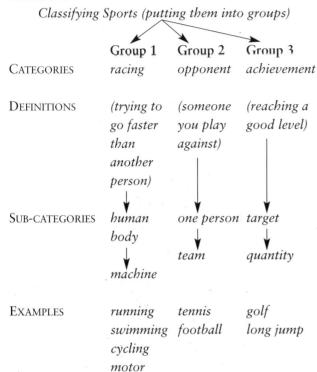

	Group 1	Group 2	Group 3
CATEGORIES	racing	opponent	achievement
DEFINITIONS	(trying to go faster than another person)	(someone you play against)	(reaching a good level)
SUB-CATEGORIES	human body ↓ machine	one person ↓ team	target ↓ quantity
EXAMPLES	running swimming cycling motor racing	tennis football	golf long jump

Exercise D

Work through the target sounds in the heading row. Set for individual work then pairwork checking. Make a copy of the table on the board or use an OHP.

If you feel the students need more help than the phonemic script can give, write an example word above each (see answers).

Answers

	1 achieve /iː/	2 have /æ/	3 car /ɑː/	4 long /ɒ/
against				
ball				
class			✓	
heard				
quantity				✓
racing				
reach	✓			
target			✓	
team	✓			
that		✓		

	5 sports /ɔː/	6 tennis /e/	7 first /ɜː/	8 play /eɪ/
against		✓		
ball	✓			
class				
heard			✓	
quantity				
racing				✓
reach				
target				
team				
that				

Closure

Get students to cover the lesson and try to redraw the classification diagram from memory, OR elicit ideas from students and recreate it on the board. Ask students to remember what the lecturer said at the end – think of more sports and classify them – and elicit another five or six sports to classify.

Play the whole lecture again. You will need to play tracks 13, 14 and 17 on CD3.

Lesson 3: Learning new skills

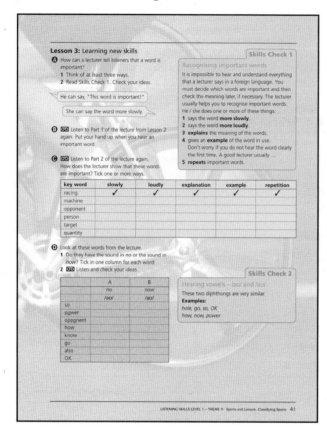

Introduction

Ask students to give you the names of some sports in each category from Lesson 2.

Possible answers
racing cycling, riding, running, motor racing
opponent football, basketball, tennis
achievement long jump, high jump, golf

Exercise A

Set for pairwork. Monitor. Feed back on 1, but don't confirm or correct. Then set reading of Skills Check 1.

Ask students to cover the Skills Check and tell you the ways a lecturer signals important words. Demonstrate each way and get students to identify it, using the bold words from the Skills Check, e.g., you say *achievement* very slowly and the students say *More slowly!*

Exercise B

Follow the procedure as written.

Exercise C

Follow the procedure as written. Feed back onto an OHT or copy on the board. Refer students to a copy of the tapescript as a final check of the way the key words are used.

Language and culture note

The meaningful value of change of pitch, speed and volume is language-specific. In other words, there is no universal that says a particular stress pattern has a particular meaning. Students therefore need to know the purpose of a particular feature in English and then to have practice identifying it in context.

Methodology note

Listeners must understand the function of language as they hear it: *Is this language important? Is this a new point or the same point said in a different way?*

Possible answers

key word	slowly	loudly	spelling	explanation	example	repetition
racing	✓	✓		✓	✓	✓
machine	✓	✓				
opponent	✓	✓				✓
person	✓	✓		✓		✓
target	✓	✓	✓	✓		✓
quantity	✓			✓	✓	

Exercise D

Give students time to try to work out the correct sound from their aural memory. Then play the recording. Before feeding back, refer students to Skills Check 2. Model the two sounds.

Finally, feed back onto the board. Write the phonemic script symbols (see Methodology note) on the board if you wish.

Answers

	A	B
	no	**now**
	/əʊ/	/aʊ/
so	✓	
p<u>o</u>wer		✓
opp<u>o</u>nent	✓	
how		✓
know	✓	
go	✓	
also	✓	
OK	✓	

Methodology note

The diphthongs are almost a combination of schwa + /uː/ and /æ/ + /uː/ respectively. You can certainly teach them in this way, i.e., *nuh oo* and *naaaaa ooo*. The two diphthongs both end in /uː/. Demonstrate this by showing how the mouth rounds to the end of each sound.

Closure

Ask students how speakers tell you that a word in a lecture is important, without looking at Skills Check 1.

Lesson 4: Applying new skills

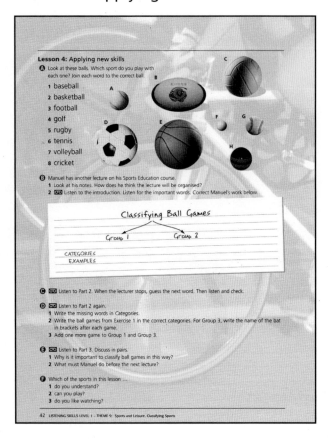

Introduction

Use Exercise A as an introduction to this lesson.

Exercise A

Students should be able to work this out by a process of elimination. If you wish, help them by describing the ball for each sport, e.g., *In golf you use a small hard white ball,* etc. If students are not sure what a particular sport is, mime the main action or get other students to explain, in English if possible. Note that the students need these sports to complete Exercise D2 below.

Answers

1	baseball G	5	rugby B
2	basketball E	6	tennis A
3	football D	7	volleyball C
4	golf F	8	cricket H

Exercise B

Note that there is space on the artwork for students to write in the missing column.

Feed back on 1 before playing the recording. Elicit some sentences that the lecturer will say if Manuel is right, e.g., *Today I'm going to talk about classifying ball games. There are two kinds of ball games.* Elicit also the kinds of ball games he could say, e.g., with one opponent or with a team.

Play the recording for students to check their ideas. Clearly, Manuel is wrong. There should be a third category.

Answers

See after Exercise D below.

Exercise C

Follow the normal procedure.

Exercise D

Make sure that students understand what they have to listen for to complete activity 2. You may need to play the recording again just for that activity.

Answers

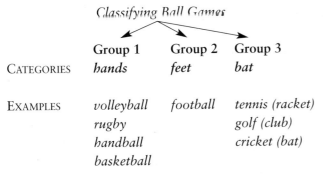

	Group 1	Group 2	Group 3
CATEGORIES	hands	feet	bat
EXAMPLES	volleyball	football	tennis (racket)
	rugby		golf (club)
	handball		cricket (bat)
	basketball		

Exercise E

Set Question 1 before playing the recording. Elicit a few ideas, but don't confirm or correct. Play the recording. Set both questions for pairwork discussion. Feed back ideas for Question 1 and games for Question 2, with their classification.

Answers

1 Because we must teach children to play at least one game in each category. This helps to develop their physical ability.
2 Classify 10 more ball games.

Exercise F and Closure

General discussion.

Play the whole lecture again. You will need to play tracks 22, 23 and 25 on CD3.

Lesson 1: Vocabulary

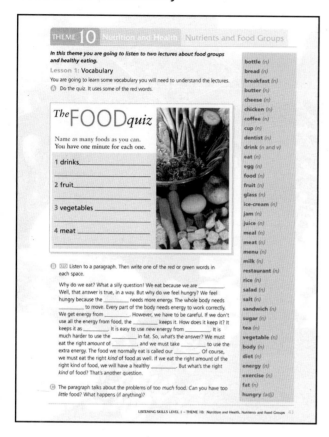

These are the phonemes that have been covered in the course to date. Take every opportunity to revise these phonemes – in addition to the set piece revision in Lesson 3:

/p/ and /b/;

/g/ and /dʒ/;

/tʃ/ and /dʒ/;

/s/ and /z/;

/t/ and /d/;

/ʃ/ , /tʃ/ , /θ/ and /ð/;

/ɪ/ and /iː/;

/æ/ and /ɑː/;

/e/ and /ə/;

/əʊ/ and /ɔː/;

/uː/;

/eɪ/, /aɪ/ and /ɔɪ/.

In addition, many of the different sounds of the letter *a* have been covered, including the sounds in:

against;

ball;

class;

heard;

quantity;

racing;

each;

target;

that.

These are the listening skills whthat have been covered in the course. Take every opportunity to revise these skills – in addition to the set piece revision of some points in Lesson 2 and Lesson 3:

* understanding spoken definitions;
* understanding spoken times;
* identifying important words;
* predicting content;
* predicting next word;
* understanding spoken spelling;
* understanding signpost language;
* following a narrative;
* following instructions;
* identifying names;
* identifying dates;
* recognising important words.

Introduction

Tell students that this unit has two purposes. Firstly, it's about nutrition and health. (Do not explain *nutrition* at this point – it will become clear during the theme – just say it's connected with food.) Secondly, it's a revision unit.

Exercise A

Put students into teams. Set each question in turn. Time the teams strictly – they can write things down, in notes or their own language. Tell the students to look at the red words and the pictures for ideas. Elicit answers from each team. Try to stop any cheating! Give one point for each correct word. Declare a winning team.

Make sure students can identify all the foods in the picture.

Answers

Answers depend on students, but make sure you elicit at least all the red words and the items depicted.

Exercise B

Set for individual work then pairwork checking. Play the recording. Students listen and follow with pens down. Then they try to copy the red and green words into the correct spaces. Remind them that the same word can be used several times.

Answers

Why do we eat? What a silly question! We eat because we are <u>hungry</u>. Well, that answer is true, in a way. But why do we feel hungry? We feel hungry because the <u>body</u> needs more energy. The whole body needs <u>energy</u> to move. Every part of the body needs energy to work correctly. We get energy from <u>food</u>. However, we have to be careful. If we don't use all the energy from food, the <u>body</u> keeps it. How does it keep it? It keeps it as <u>fat</u>. It is easy to use *new* energy from <u>food</u>. It is much harder to use the <u>energy</u> in fat. So, what's the answer? We must eat the right *amount* of <u>food</u>, and we must take <u>exercise</u> to use the extra energy. The food we normally eat is called our <u>diet</u>. Of course, we must eat the right *kind* of food as well. If we eat the right amount of the right kind of food, we will have a healthy <u>diet</u>. But what's the right *kind* of food? That's another question.

Exercise C

General discussion. This could be very short with mention of illness from lack of particular items, or could perhaps lead on to talk about anorexia and unnecessary dieting. See how it goes.

Closure

Say 10 red and green words. Ask students to number them in the order you say them. If you wish, repeat the activity with a different 10 words but this time in context. These activities practice the vital listening skills of hearing words in isolation and in the stream of speech.

Lesson 2: Listening review (1)

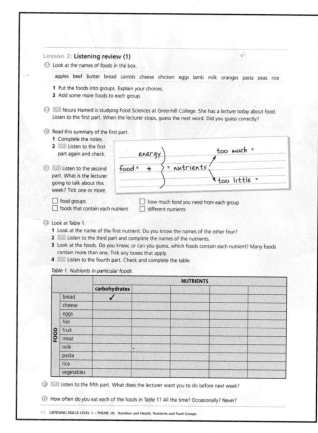

Language and culture note

There is no concept in Arabic similar to the English countable / uncountable distinction. You need to deal with it therefore like any other grammar point – i.e., language-specific not some universal truth. Arabic speakers have no difficulty with the concept of *foods* therefore, even though the word sounds somewhat specialised to a native speaker.

Exercise A

Set for pairwork. Point out that they may know a name for some of the groups and not for others. Feed back onto the board. Do not provide the names for the ? groups. They will learn the names in this unit.

Answers
Possible items:

name of group	food items	extras depend on students
fruit	apples; oranges	
vegetables	carrots; peas	
meat	chicken; beef; lamb	
????	bread; pasta; rice	
????	milk; cheese; butter; eggs*	

*Students may put eggs in a different category.

Exercise B

Follow the normal procedure for this activity.

Exercise C

Set for individual work then pairwork checking. Play Part 1 twice. Feed back by building up the notes on the board. Then students tell you what they mean.

Language and culture note

The information about chemicals is not as difficult as it might seem for Arabic speakers. The word *kemia* means chemicals; the elements *magnesium* and *calcium* sound almost the same in Arabic.

Introduction

Elicit the names of as many foods and drinks as you can. Perhaps try the Alphabet of Food and Drink game, i.e., *Can you think of a food beginning with …?*

A   apple; apricot
B   butter; beef; bread
C   cheese; chicken; carrots; coffee
D   dates
E   eggs
F   fish
G   greens, i.e., vegetables (same in Arabic!)

It doesn't matter if they can't think of one. Just move on to the next letter, OR give letters at random where you know there is a well-known food / drink.

Point out that the word *food* is normally uncountable. But like most uncountable words in English, we can make it plural if we are talking about different types of the thing – i.e., different foods. (The same thing happens with coffees, sugars, etc.)

Methodology note

By now, students should be used to picking up the meanings of words from the lecture itself. So the new words are not specifically focussed on here. However, you can highlight them if you wish. The point is revised specifically in the next lesson.

Answer

food = energy + chemicals) > = nutrients < too much = fat / too little = ill

Exercise D

Give students time to look at the possible topics. Set for individual work then pairwork checking. Play Part 2.

Answers

... food groups
✓ foods that contain each nutrient
... how much food you need from each group
✓ different nutrients

Exercise E

Give students time to understand the table. Set for individual work then pairwork checking. Play Part 3. Feed back onto an OHT or the board.

Play Part 4. Feed back as before.

Language and culture note

The following words from this section are similar in sound in Arabic:

carbohydrate protein vitamin

Of course, the fact that it is the same word in the students' own language does not necessarily mean that the students know what it is or means!

Answers

Table 1: Nutrients in particular foods

	carbohydrates	protein	vitamins	fats	minerals
bread	✓				
cheese		✓		✓	
eggs					✓
fish		✓		✓	
fruit			✓		
meat		✓		✓	✓
milk				✓	✓
pasta	✓				
rice	✓				
vegetables			✓		

(NUTRIENTS across the top; FOOD down the side)

Exercise F

Set for pairwork. Play Part 5. Feed back orally. Set the actual task for the students to do if it is feasible. There are conflicting points about food groups but they should be able to find out the basics.

Answer

Look up food groups on the Internet. Make some notes of different ideas.

Exercise G

General discussion or pairwork.

Closure

Get students to cover the lesson and try to redraw the table of nutrients in different foods from memory, OR elicit ideas from students and recreate it on the board.

Play the whole lecture again. You will need to play tracks 27 and 29–32 on CD3.

Lesson 3: Listening review (2)

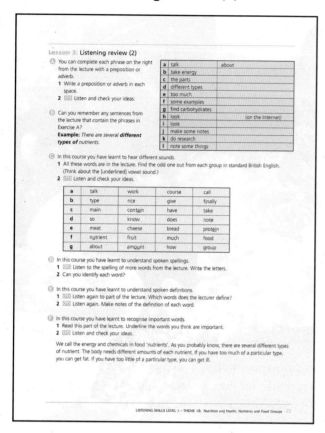

some examples   of
find carbohydrates   in
look   at
look   up (on the Internet)
make some notes   of
do research   on
note some things   down

Exercise B

Elicit a few ideas. Encourage as many students as possible to contribute.

Methodology note

Don't worry too much about the pronunciation, since this is the skill of listening not speaking; as long as it is intelligible, they are proving that they heard the phrase in the stream of speech.

Introduction

Say some foods from the first two lessons and get students to categorise them. For the moment, you will only be able to do fruits, vegetables, drinks and meat. *Dairy products* has not been taught and the idea that bread, pasta, rice, etc., can be called *carbohydrates* has not been specifically taught.

Exercise A

Set for pairwork. Play the lecture. Feed back by getting the phrases on the board.

Answers

talk   about
take energy   from
the parts   of
different types   of
too much   of

Exercise C

Make sure students understand that they have to pick out the word with the different vowel sound. Go through the first set as an example. Set for pairwork. Play the recording for students to check.

Answers
Odd one out in bold italics.

a   talk *work* course call
b   type rice *give* finally
c   main contain *have* take
d   so know *does* note
e   meat cheese *bread** protein
f   nutrient fruit *much* food
g   about amount how *group*

Note: The wrong word, *need* is recorded on the tapescript. Read these four words to students for them to pick the odd one (*bread*).

Exercise D

Set for individual work then pairwork checking. Play the recording. Feed back by getting students to dictate the words back to you for writing on the board.

Answers

human
nutrient
chemicals
orange
carrot
pasta
body
finally
energy

Closure

Elicit some of the phrases again from Exercise A.

Exercise E

Set for individual work then pairwork checking. Play the recording twice, once for word and once for definition. Feed back orally.

Answers

energy	the ability to do work
chemicals	things like calcium and magnesium
nutrients	energy and chemicals in food

Exercise F

Remind students of some of the ways that you can recognise important words – particularly, in this case, the lecturer speaking more loudly and more slowly. Set for individual work then pairwork checking. Play the recording. Play it again if necessary.

Answers

We call the energy and chemicals in food ‘<u>nutrients</u>’. As you probably know, there are several different <u>types</u> of nutrient. The body needs <u>different amounts</u> of each nutrient. If you have <u>too much</u> of a particular type, you can get <u>fat</u>. If you have too little of a particular type, you can get <u>ill</u>.

Lesson 4: Listening review (3)

Introduction

Use Exercise A as an introduction to this lesson.

Exercise A

Write the words on the board. As you start to write, get students to complete the words. Set for pairwork.

Feed back by marking the order of some of the pairs on the board. Do not confirm or correct – it is the main content point of the lesson.

Note, like *foods*, *fats* is countable when it means *types of fat*.

Exercise B

Follow the normal procedure.

Exercise C

Set for individual work then pairwork checking. Feed back by building up the notes on the board.

Answers
Additional points in italics
1. food *groups* = a group of *foods* = 6; some are the same as *nutrients*, some are diff.
2. healthy eating = groups together in *healthy* way
3. own *diet*

Exercise D

Set the question in 1. Give students some time to discuss it. Then play Part 2. Elicit answers.

Answers
Food groups are the ones in A except eggs, milk and cheese = dairy products.

Exercise E

Give students plenty of time to study the figure. Make sure they understand that the one square in place indicates the amount of fats you should have. Elicit how the completed figure should look – do not confirm, but correct any misunderstandings about the way it is constructed and / or labelled.

Play the recording. Deal with the word *portion*. It means a small amount. Explain that you can get a definition of a small amount of each of these foods on the Internet. The word *serving* is also used.

Monitor and if necessary play the recording again when they understand what to do. Feed back on an OHT or build up the figure on the board. Make sure students can correctly interpret the figure – i.e., work out the order in terms of quantity of portions.

Point out that this is one idea of a balanced diet. There are others. Specifically there are fashions in what is a balanced diet as new research becomes available. The students should do their own research to find out a range of ideas and decide which they accept before acting on it.

Answer

Figure 1: The balanced diet pyramid

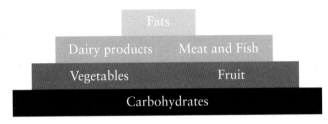

Order in terms of portions

	Portions	%
Fats	1	5
Meat and fish	2	10
Dairy products / Fruit	3	15
Vegetables	4	20
Carbohydrates	10	50
Total portions	20	

Exercise F

Set for individual work then pairwork checking. Play the last part. Feed back orally.

Answer
Think about your own diet and make a diet pyramid.

Exercise G

Set for individual work – in class or for homework.

Closure

Get the students to turn the information about number of portions into a pie chart, based on the percentages in the answer to Exercise E above.

Play the whole lecture again. You will need to play tracks 39, 41, 42 and 44 on CD3.

THEME 1
Education, Student Life

answer (n and v)

ask (v)

begin (v)

dictionary (n)

end (v)

explain (v)

history (n)

learn (v)

listen (v)

mathematics (n)

question (n)

read (v)

right (adj)

science (n)

spell (v)

student (n)

study (v)

teach (v)

test (n and v)

university (n)

write (v)

wrong (adj)

academic (adj)

college (n)

head (n)

in charge (of) (adj)

lecture (n)

principal (n)

responsible (for) (adj)

semester (n)

subject (n)

term (n)

THEME 2
Daily Life, Schedules

afternoon (n)

autumn (n)

day (n)

evening (n)

first (adj)

hour (n)

last (adj)

late (adj)

later (adj)

midnight (n)

minute (n)

month (n)

morning (n)

night (n)

noon (n)

now (adv)

o'clock (adv)

past (adv and n)

quarter (n)

spring (n)

summer (n)

time (n)

today (n)

tomorrow (n)

tonight (n)

week (n)

winter (n)

year (n)

yesterday (n)

campus (n)

chess (n)

club (n)

film (n)

music (n)

plan (v)

restaurant (n)

sports (n)

THEME 3
Work and Business, Work Starts Now!

company (n)

computer (n)

desk (n)

e-mail (n)

envelope (n)

factory (n)

file (n)

job (n)

letter (n)

manager (n)

office (n)

secretary (n)

shelf / shelves (n)

shop (n)

start (v)

supermarket (n)

typist (n)

website (n)

work (n and v)

working hours (n)

colleague (n)

papers (n)

product (n)

rely on (v)

salary (n)

service (n)

urgent (adj)

THEME 4
Science and Nature, So You Want to Be a Scientist?

black (adj)

blue (adj)

brown (adj)

cold (adj)

colour (n and v)

cloud (n)

flower (n)

fog (n)

forest (n)

grass (n)

green (adj)

grey (adj)

hot (adj)

island (n)

lake (n)

mountain (n)

orange (adj)

rain (n and v)

red (adj)

river (n)

sea (n)

sky (n)

snow (n and v)

sun (n)

temperature (n)

thunderstorm (n)

tree (n)

water (n)

weather (n)

white (adj)

wind (n)

yellow (adj)

graph (n)

laboratory (n)

science (n)

scientific (adj)

scientist (n)

table (n)

test (v)

THEME 5
The Physical World, Where Is Your Country?

behind *(prep)*

between *(prep)*

corner *(n)*

country *(n)*

east *(n)*

in front of *(prep)*

in the centre of *(prep)*

left *(n)*

mountain *(n)*

near *(prep)*

next to *(prep)*

north *(n)*

opposite *(prep)*

south *(n)*

town *(n)*

west *(n)*

border *(n and v)*

continent *(n)*

locate *(v)*

location *(n)*

the Equator *(n)*

the Tropic of Cancer *(n)*

the Tropic of Capricorn *(n)*

THEME 6
Culture and Civilization, Congratulations!

adult *(n)*

age *(n)*

be born *(v)*

boy *(n)*

child *(n)*

congratulations *(n)*

dead *(adj)*

die *(v)*

family *(n)*

friend *(n)*

girl *(n)*

group *(n)*

guest *(n)*

live *(v)*

man *(n)*

married *(adj)*

name *(n)*

old *(adj)*

party *(n)*

people *(n)*

person *(n)*

present *(n)*

single *(adj)*

thank *(v)*

thank you *(interj)*

woman *(n)*

celebrate *(v)*

celebration *(n)*

ceremony *(n)*

event *(n)*

festival *(n)*

special *(adj)*

take place *(v)*

traditional *(adj)*

THEME 7
They Made Our World, Who? What? When?

accident *(n)*

airport *(n)*

arrive *(v)*

bicycle *(n)*

boat *(n)*

bus *(n)*

bus stop *(n)*

car *(n)*

come *(v)*

drive *(v)*

driver *(n)*

fly *(v)*

go *(v)*

land *(v)*

leave *(v)*

passenger *(n)*

pilot *(n)*

plane *(n)*

road *(n)*

sail *(v)*

sailor *(n)*

ship *(n)*

street *(n)*

take off *(v)*

traffic *(n)*

train *(n)*

in the air *(prep)*

invent *(v)*

invention *(n)*

on land *(prep)*

on the sea *(prep)*

ride *(v)*

track *(n)*

transport *(n)*

travel *(v)*

THEME 8
Art and Literature, There Was Once a Poor Man …

bring *(v)*

build *(v)*

carry *(v)*

check *(v)*

climb *(v)*

come *(v)*

do *(v)*

draw *(v)*

end *(v)*

feel *(v)*

find *(v)*

get *(v)*

give *(v)*

go *(v)*

leave *(v)*

live *(v)*

look *(v)*

make *(v)*

meet *(v)*

move *(v)*

point *(v)*

put *(v)*

run *(v)*

say *(v)*

send *(v)*

start *(v)*

stop *(v)*

take *(v)*

talk *(v)*

tell *(v)*

walk *(v)*

want *(v)*

appear *(v)*

character *(n)*

literature *(n)*

moral *(n)*

stories *(n)*

story *(n)*

translate *(v)*

writer *(n)*

THEME 9
Sports and Leisure, Classifying Sports

ball (n)

baseball (n)

beach (n)

film (n and v)

football (n)

hobby (n)

magazine (n)

news (n)

newspaper (n)

play (n and v)

programme (n)

radio (n)

show (n)

sport (n)

sports (n)

swimming (n)

tennis (n)

theatre (n)

turn off (v)

turn on (v)

watch (v)

cycling (n)

equipment (n)

golf (n)

ice hockey (n)

player (n)

riding (n)

rugby (n)

running (n)

team (n)

THEME 10
Nutrition and Health, Nutrients and Food Groups

bottle (n)

bread (n)

breakfast (n)

butter (n)

cheese (n)

chicken (n)

coffee (n)

cup (n)

dentist (n)

drink (n and v)

eat (n)

egg (n)

food (n)

fruit (n)

glass (n)

ice-cream (n)

jam (n)

juice (n)

meal (n)

meat (n)

menu (n)

milk (n)

restaurant (n)

rice (n)

salad (n)

salt (n)

sandwich (n)

sugar (n)

tea (n)

vegetable (n)

body (n)

diet (n)

energy (n)

exercise (n)

fat (n)

hungry (adj)

academic (adj)

accident (n)

adult (n)

afternoon (n)

age (n)

airport (n)

answer (n and v)

appear (v)

arrive (v)

ask (v)

autumn (n)

ball (n)

baseball (n)

be born (v)

beach (n)

begin (v)

behind (prep)

between (prep)

bicycle (n)

black (adj)

blue (adj)

boat (n)

body (n)

border (n and v)

bottle (n)

boy (n)

bread (n)

breakfast (n)

bring (v)

brown (adj)

build (v)

bus (n)

bus stop (n)

butter (n)

campus (n)

car (n)

carry (v)

celebrate (v)

celebration (n)

ceremony (n)

character (n)

check (v)

cheese (n)

chess (n)

chicken (n)

child (n)

climb (v)

cloud (n)

club (n)

coffee (n)

cold (adj)

colleague (n)

college (n)

colour (n and v)

come (v)

company (n)

computer (n)

congratulations (n)

continent (n)

corner (n)

country (n)

cup (n)

cycling (n)

day (n)

dead (adj)

dentist (n)

desk (n)

dictionary (n)

die (v)

diet (n)

do (v)

draw (v)

drink (n and v)

drive (v)

driver (n)

east (n)

eat (n)

egg (n)

e-mail (n)

end (v)

energy (n)

envelope (n)

equipment (n)

evening (n)

event (n)	in the air (prep)	mountain (n)	rely on (v)
exercise (n)	in the centre of	move (v)	responsible (for) (adj)
explain (v)	(prep)	music (n)	restaurant (n)
factory (n)	invent (v)	name (n)	rice (n)
family (n)	invention (n)	near (prep)	ride (v)
fat (n)	island (n)	news (n)	riding (n)
feel (v)	jam (n)	newspaper (n)	right (adj)
festival (n)	job (n)	next to (prep)	river (n)
file (n)	juice (n)	night (n)	road (n)
film (n and v)	laboratory (n)	noon (n)	rugby (n)
find (v)	lake (n)	north (n)	run (v)
first (adj)	land (v)	now (adj)	running (n)
flower (n)	last (adj)	o'clock (adv)	sail (v)
fly (v)	late (adj)	office (n)	sailor (n)
fog (n)	later (adj)	old (adj)	salad (n)
food (n)	learn (v)	on land (prep)	salary (n)
football (n)	leave (v)	on the sea (prep)	salt (n)
forest (n)	lecture (n)	opposite (prep)	sandwich (n)
friend (n)	left (n)	orange (adj)	say (v)
fruit (n)	letter (n)	papers (n)	science (n)
get (v)	listen (v)	party (n)	science (n)
girl (n)	literature (n)	passenger (n)	scientific (adj)
give (v)	live (v)	past (adv and n)	scientist (n)
glass (n)	locate (v)	people (n)	sea (n)
go (v)	location (n)	person (n)	secretary (n)
golf (n)	look (v)	pilot (n)	semester (n)
graph (n)	magazine (n)	plan (n)	send (v)
grass (n)	make (v)	plane (n)	service (n)
green (adj)	man (n)	play (n and v)	shelf / shelves (n)
grey (adj)	manager (n)	player (n)	ship (n)
group (n)	married (adj)	point (v)	shop (n)
guest (n)	mathematics (n)	present (n)	show (n)
head (n)	meal (n)	principal (n)	single (adj)
history (n)	meat (n)	product (n)	sky (n)
hobby (n)	meet (v)	programme (n)	snow (n and v)
hot (adj)	menu (n)	put (v)	south (n)
hour (n)	midnight (n)	quarter (n)	special (adj)
hungry (adj)	milk (n)	question (n)	spell (v)
ice hockey (n)	minute (n)	radio (n)	sport (n)
ice-cream (n)	month (n)	rain (n and v)	sports (n)
in charge (of) (adj)	moral (n)	read (v)	sports (n)
in front of (prep)	morning (n)	red (adj)	spring (n)

start (v)

stop (v)

stories (n)

story (n)

street (n)

student (n)

study (v)

subject (n)

sugar (n)

summer (n)

sun (n)

supermarket (n)

swimming (n)

table (n)

take off (v)

take place (v)

talk (v)

tea (n)

teach (v)

team (n)

tell (v)

temperature (n)

tennis (n)

term (n)

test (n and v)

test (v)

thank (v)

thank you (interj)

theatre (n)

the Equator (n)

the Tropic of
Cancer (n)

the Tropic of
Capricorn (n)

thunderstorm (n)

time (n)

today (n)

tomorrow (n)

tonight (n)

town (n)

track (n)

traditional (adj)

traffic (n)

train (n)

translate (v)

transport (n)

travel (v)

tree (n)

turn off (v)

turn on (v)

typist (n)

university (n)

urgent (adj)

vegetable (n)

walk (v)

want (v)

watch (v)

water (n)

weather (n)

website (n)

week (n)

west (n)

white (adj)

wind (n)

winter (n)

woman (n)

work (n and v)

working hours (n)

write (v)

writer (n)

wrong (adj)

year (n)

yellow (adj)

yesterday (n)

Tapescript

Presenter:	Theme 1: Education, Student Life
	Lesson 1: Vocabulary
	B Listen to some sentences with the green words. Then complete each sentence with one of the words.
Voice:	1 The academic year in my country starts in October. All the students go back to high school then.
	2 When does the second semester start? Is it in February?
	3 Which room is the lecture in? The one about learning English?
	4 Mr Jones is in charge of the library. He is responsible for all the books and CD-ROMs.
	5 Who is the head of Year 1? Is it Mrs Wright? Or is she in charge of Year 2?

Presenter:	**Lesson 2: Listening**
	C It is the start of the college year at Greenhill College. The principal is welcoming the new students. Listen and add the missing information.
Peter Bean:	OK. Let's begin. Welcome to Greenhill College. I am very pleased to see you all here.
	My name is Peter Bean. I'm the principal – that means I am in charge of the whole place. You come and see me if you have any problems with the fees – that means the money you must pay. My office is on the first floor, Room 15, by the stairs. The people behind me are some of my staff. This is Mrs Polly Penn. She's the head of Year 1. She is responsible for the schedule. After this meeting, Mrs Penn will give you the schedule for the first term. The schedule tells you the times of all your lectures. Mrs Penn will also give you the name of your instructor. We call the teachers at Greenhill instructors. She will also tell you the name of your personal advisor*** – that's a person who helps you if you have problems. Finally, this is the registrar, Mr Bill Beale. He's in charge of attendance. If you can't come to college one day, tell Mr Beale. OK, that's it from me. Now I'll hand over to Mrs Penn … Oh, I nearly forgot. Mr Beale's room is on the first floor, next to my room – Room 16.

| Presenter: | **E The principal explains the meaning of each word in Exercise D. Listen to his speech again and check your answers.** |
| | [REPEAT OF LESSON 2 EXERCISE C] |

Presenter:	**Lesson 3: Learning new skills**
	A Listen and tick the words you hear. If you get three ticks in a line, say Bingo!
	[REPEAT OF LESSON 2 EXERCISE C]

Presenter:	**B 2 Listen and check your answers.**
Voice:	pay – letter p
	Bill – letter b
	Penn – letter p
	personal – letter p
	Bean – letter b
	Peter – letter p
	people – letter p
	place – letter p
	pleased – letter p

Beale – letter b
Polly – letter p
principal – letter p
problems – letter p
behind – letter b

Presenter:	**B 3 Listen to these words connected with education. Is the missing letter *p* or *b*?**
Voice:	a book
	b paper
	c begin
	d spell
	e pass
	f period
	g subject
	h explain

Presenter:	**C 2 Look at these pairs of words. Listen. Which do you hear in each case? Don't worry about the meanings.**
Voice:	a hill
	b steal
	c will
	d meal
	e pill
	f kill
	g feel
	h feet
	i Bill
	j beat

Presenter:	**D Listen to the first part of the principal's speech again. It's much slower this time. Put your left hand up every time you hear *p*. Put your right hand up every time you hear *b*.**
Peter Bean:	OK. Let's begin. Welcome to Greenhill College. I am very pleased to see you all here. My name is Peter Bean. I'm the principal. You come and see me if you have any problems with the fees – that means the money you must pay. My office is on the first floor, Room 15, by the stairs. The people behind me are some of my staff. This is Mrs Polly Penn. She's the head of Year 1. She is responsible for the schedule. After this meeting, Mrs Penn will give you the schedule for the first term. The schedule tells you the times of all your lectures.

Presenter:	**E Listen to the second part of the speech again. Say *i* every time you hear the short sound. Say *ee* every time you hear the long sound.**
Peter Bean:	Mrs Penn will also give you the name of your instructor. We call the teachers at Greenhill instructors. She will also tell you the name of your personal advisor – that's a person who helps you if you have problems. Finally, this is the registrar, Mr Bill Beale. He's in charge of attendance. If you can't come to the college one day, tell Mr Beale. OK, that's it from me. Now I'll hand over to Mrs Penn … Oh, I nearly forgot. Mr Beale's room is on the first floor, next to my room – Room 16.

Presenter:	**Lesson 4: Applying new skills** **B Listen to some sentences from the principal's speech in Lesson 2. What is Mrs Penn going to talk about? Tick one or more topic.**
Peter Bean:	This is Mrs Polly Penn. She's the head of Year 1. She is responsible for the schedule. After this meeting, Mrs Penn will give you the schedule for the first term. The schedule tells you the times of all your lectures. Mrs Penn will also give you the name of your instructor.

	We call the teachers at Greenhill instructors. She will also tell you the name of your personal advisor – that's a person who helps you if you have problems.

Presenter:	**C Listen to Mrs Penn's speech. Underline the topics to check your answers to Exercise B.**
Polly Penn:	OK. First, your schedule. In the first term, you do General Studies and English. General Studies means subjects like religion, maths, science and the arts. So, every day, you do three periods of General Studies in the morning and three of English in the afternoon. If you have any problems with any of your studies, go and see your personal advisor. The advisors' rooms are on the third floor. Now, listen carefully. If your surname – I mean your family name – begins with A, B, C, D or E, your advisor is Mrs Piper. If your surname begins with F, G, H, I or J, your advisor is Mrs Barber. If your surname begins with K, L, M, N or O, your advisor is Mrs Peebles. If your surname begins with P, Q, R, S or T, your advisor is Mrs Bream. If your surname begins with U, V, W, X, Y or Z, your advisor is Mrs Pinner.

Presenter:	**D Imagine you are a new student at Greenhill College.** **1 Listen to the first part of Mrs Penn's speech again. Which schedule above is correct for you?**
Polly Penn:	OK. First, your schedule. In the first term, you have two subjects. You do General Studies and English. You have three periods of General Studies in the morning and three periods of English in the afternoon. General Studies means subjects like religion, maths, science and the arts.

Presenter:	**2 Listen to the second part of Mrs Penn's speech again. What is the name of your personal advisor? Tick one.**
Polly Penn:	If you have any problems with any of your studies, go and see your personal advisor. The advisors' rooms are on the third floor. Now, listen carefully. If your surname – I mean your family name – begins with A, B, C, D or E, your advisor is Mrs Piper. If your surname begins with F, G, H, I or J, your advisor is Mrs Barber. If your surname begins with K, L, M, N or O, your advisor is Mrs Peebles. If your surname begins with P, Q, R, S or T, your advisor is Mrs Bream. If your surname begins with U, V, W, X, Y or Z, your advisor is Mrs Pinner.

Presenter:	**Theme 2: Daily Life, Schedules** **Lesson 1: Vocabulary** **C Listen to some sentences with the green words. Number the words in order.**
Voice:	1 There is a very good restaurant in North Road. The food is excellent.
	2 I don't like chess. In fact, I don't like any games like that.
	3 Do you play any sports? Football, basketball, handball?
	4 My sister is excellent at music. She plays the piano, the flute and the guitar.
	5 Have you joined the college computer club yet?
	6 This university has a very big campus – there are about twenty college buildings and several houses for students to live in.

7 It is very important to plan your day. Make sure there is time for college work and family life.

8 I watched the new Indian film at the cinema yesterday.

Presenter: **Lesson 2: Listening**
C Listen to Mrs Penn's definitions and check your answers.

Mrs Penn: a I'm going to give you your schedule – that's the days and times of your classes – for this semester, OK?
b First I want you to write the start time and the end time of each period – in other words, each part of the day.
c Lunch is served in the cafeteria – that's the restaurant on the campus.
d You have a short recess – I mean, a short break between classes.

Presenter: **D Mrs Penn is going to give you your schedule. Listen and answer these questions.**

Mrs Penn: OK. Is everybody ready? Have you all got a pencil? Good. I'm going to give you your schedule – that's the days and times of your classes – for this semester, OK? Can you fill it in as I read it out? If you're not sure about anything, ask your friends after this talk. OK. First I want you to write the start time and the end time of each period – in other words, each part of the day. As you can see, there are six periods, three in the morning and three in the afternoon. There's also a lunch period which lasts an hour. Lunch is served in the cafeteria – that's the restaurant on the campus. OK. Each period is one hour, so that's three hours in the morning and … how many hours in the afternoon?

Student 1: Three.
Mrs Penn: Good. The first period begins at 9 o'clock. So can you write 9 o'clock in the first morning space? When does the first period end?
Student 2: Half past nine.
Mrs Penn: No, not half past nine.
Student 3: 9.45?
Mrs Penn: No! Come on, think!
Student 1: 10 o'clock.
Mrs Penn: Why?
Student 1: Because each period is one hour.
Mrs Penn: Right. Good. So the next period begins at 10 o'clock, right?
Student 1: Yes.
Mrs Penn: Wrong. You have a short recess – I mean, a short break between classes. The recess is 10 minutes long. So the next period begins at …?
Student 2: Five past ten.
Student 3: Ten past ten.
Mrs Penn: That's right. OK. So now you can fill in the other times …

Presenter: **E Listen again.**
[REPEAT OF LESSON 2 EXERCISE D]

Presenter: **F 2 Listen and check your ideas.**
Voice: a each   column 2
b give   column 1
c mean   column 2
d read   column 2
e see   column 2
f six   column 1
g this   column 1
h three   column 2
i begins   column 1
j between column 2

Presenter: **G 2 Listen and check your ideas.**
Voice: a about   letter b
b because letter b
c begins   letter b
d pencil   letter p
e between letter p
f break   letter b
g space   letter p
h campus   letter p
i part   letter p
j period   letter p

Presenter: **Lesson 3: Learning new skills**
B 1 Listen to eight times. Letter the clocks A to H.
Voice: c six o'clock
f ten past eight
b quarter past seven
d twenty past four
g half past eleven
a twenty to ten
h quarter to three
e It's ten to four.

Presenter: **3 Listen to the times again and check.**
[REPEAT OF LESSON 3 EXERCISE B1]

Presenter: **C 3 Listen and check your ideas.**
Mrs Penn: a Have you all got a pencil?
b ask your friends
c after this talk
d the start time
e each part of the day
f in the afternoon
g it lasts an hour
h in the cafeteria
i on the campus
j half past nine

Presenter: **Lesson 4: Applying new skills**
C Mrs Penn runs the extracurricular activities at Greenhill College. Listen and find out:
1 the meaning of *extracurricular*;
2 the extracurricular activities at the college – tick the activities on the notice board.

Mrs Penn: OK, so that's the schedule. Now, some other information for you. We have extracurricular activities – that means extra things you can do after college work every evening, so can you make a note of these? If you want to do any of the activities, just come along to the first meeting this week. Right. First, we have Sports Club on Saturday at 8 o'clock in the evening – you can do basketball, handball, table tennis and lots of other sports. Then there's Film Night on Sunday, starting at 8.30. We have a different film every week and after the film, there's a discussion. It's Quiz Time on Monday. Come with a friend and take part in a General Knowledge quiz. That starts at a quarter of eight. Computer Club is on Tuesday. It doesn't matter whether you are a beginner or an expert. Come and learn or just have fun. Computer Club starts at a quarter after eight. Finally, we have Music Makers on Wednesday night. If you play an instrument or want to learn, join the music makers at half past seven. I'll run through those again in case you missed anything.

Presenter: **D Listen again and write in the days and times for each activity that you ticked.**
[REPEAT OF LESSON 4 EXERCISE C]

Presenter:	**Theme 3: Work and Business, Work Starts Now!**
	Lesson 1: Vocabulary
	B Listen to some sentences with the green words. Then complete each sentence.
Voice:	1 People don't like him at work. They can't rely on him. They never know if he will be late, or not come to work at all.
	2 It is very important to have good colleagues to work with in a job.
	3 That work isn't urgent. You can do it tomorrow.
	4 Where are the papers for my next meeting? Are they in the file?
	5 If you are paid every month, we call that money salary.
	6 Some companies make products – real things like computers, televisions or cars.
	7 Some companies give services — like banks, cleaning companies or car hire companies.

Presenter:	**Lesson 2: Listening**
	B Gerald Gardiner is a management consultant. He is at Greenhill College today. He is talking to the first-year students about work. Listen to the first part of his talk.
	1 How many points does he make?
	2 Can you remember any of the points?
Gerald Gardiner:	How do you get a good job when you leave college? You start thinking about it NOW! Change the way that you think about college. Think of college as a job – your job. You will find it much easier then to live in the world of work in two or three years' time.
	So college should be a job. But what is a job? What must you do in a job? I'm going to tell you nine things.
	Number 1: You must go to work every day.
	Number 2: You must be punctual – that means, you must always be on time.
	Number 3: You must respect your manager – the person who gives you orders – and your colleagues – that is, the people you work with.
	Number 4: You must also respect the customers, in other words, the people who buy things from the company.
	Number 5: You must do all the tasks or pieces of work that your manager gives you.
	Number 6: You must complete all your tasks on time.
	Number 7: You are responsible for the quality of your work – whether it is good or bad.
	Number 8: You must keep your workplace tidy – your desk, and any shelves or cupboards that you use.
	Number 9: You must organise your work files sensibly – in alphabetical order or chronologically – in other words, by date.

Presenter:	**C Listen again. How does he define these words? Match each word to a definition.**
	[REPEAT OF LESSON 2 EXERCISE B]

Presenter:	**E Listen again and check your answers.**
	[REPEAT OF LESSON 2 EXERCISE B]

Presenter:	**F 2 Listen and check your ideas.**
Voice:	are column D
	bad column C
	colleagues column B
	gives column A
	keep column B
	leave column B
	manager column C
	people column B
	pieces column B

	start column D
	that column C
	think column A

Presenter:	**G 2 Listen and check your ideas.**
Voice:	a punctual letter p
	b respect letter p
	c buy letter b
	d pieces letter p
	e sensibly letter b
	f people letter p
	g job letter b
	h company letter p
	i responsible letter p
	j workplace letter p
	k complete letter p
	l person letter p

Presenter:	**Lesson 3: Learning new skills**
	B 2 Listen and check your ideas.
Voice:	a You must go to work every day.
	b You must be punctual.
	c You must respect your manager and your colleagues.
	d You must also respect the customers.
	e You must do all the tasks or pieces of work that your manager gives you.
	f You must complete all your tasks on time.
	g You are responsible for the quality of your work.
	h You must keep your workplace tidy.
	i You must organise your work files sensibly.

Presenter:	**C 2 Listen and check your answers.**
Voice:	go row A
	give row A
	college row B
	get row A
	change row B
	colleague row A
	organise row A

Presenter:	**4 Listen and check your answers.**
Voice:	age row B
	page row B
	begin row A
	charge row B
	ago row A
	again row A
	large row B
	big row A

Presenter:	**6 Listen and check your answers.**
Voice:	danger row B
	angry row A
	wage row B
	magazine row A
	rig row A

Presenter:	**Lesson 4: Applying new skills**
	D 1 Listen and write one or two stressed words under *Gerald's reasons* in the blue table. Guess the spelling.
Gerald Gardiner:	Why must you do all these things in a job? Let's look at each thing and suggest a reason.
	You must go to work every day. Why? Because people rely on you. They need you to do your work so they can do their work.
	You must be punctual. Why? Because people expect you at a certain time. If you are late, you waste their time.

You must respect your manager and your colleagues. Why? Because you have to work together every day. You must respect the customers. Why? Because, in the end, they pay your wages.

You must do all the tasks that your manager gives you. Why? Because all jobs have interesting tasks and boring tasks, easy tasks and difficult tasks.

You must complete all your tasks on time. Why? Because other people need the information.

You are responsible for the quality of your work. Why? Because it is very bad for a company if a customer is dissatisfied with a product or service.

You must keep your workplace tidy. Why? Because it is rude to make other people put up with your mess.

You must organise your work files sensibly. Why? Because you might be ill one day. Then a manager or colleague will have to find urgent papers in your work files.

Presenter: 2 **Listen again. Make notes on Gerald's reasons where you have a cross. Listen for the important words.**
[REPEAT OF LESSON 4 EXERCISE D]

Presenter: **Theme 4: Science and Nature, So You Want to Be a Scientist?**
Lesson 1: Vocabulary
C **Listen to a paragraph. Then write one of the green words in each space.**
Voice: Science is the study of how things work in the world. A scientist usually works in a laboratory. He or she tests things to find out the facts. He or she often puts the facts in a table, with columns of information, or in a graph, with blocks or lines that represent the information.

Presenter: **Lesson 2: Listening**
C 1 **Listen to the introduction to the programme. Tick each point in the programme information when Arthur mentions it.**
Arthur Burns: This week on *So you want to be...* we are looking at the job of the scientist. What is science? What do scientists do? What is scientific method? And the most important question of all: Is science the right career for you?

Presenter: 2 **Listen to the first part of the programme. Put your hand up when Arthur starts to talk about a new point.**
Arthur Burns: First, what is science? Science is the study of how things work in the world. The word *science* comes from Greek and Latin words meaning 'to know'. What do scientists do? Well, scientists are not satisfied just to *think* something is true. They must *prove* it. *Proving* means showing that something is always true. In this way, scientists are different from other people. Let me show you the difference.
I know that plants need sunlight and water to live. At least, I think that's true. But thinking is not enough for a scientist. If a scientist *thinks* something is true, he or she wants to *prove* it.
How can scientists prove that something is true? They must follow the scientific method. A method is a way of doing something. But what is the scientific method? It works like this: Firstly, a scientist makes a hypothesis, which means an idea of the truth. Then he or she tests the hypothesis. Scientists can test hypotheses in two main ways. They can do an experiment, which means a test in a laboratory. Scientists study what happens during the experiment. Or they can do research, which

means looking up information. They usually do research in a library or, nowadays, on the Internet. With research, scientists look at what happened in the past.
In both cases – experiments and research – they collect data. Data is information before it is organised. Then they display the results in a table or a graph. Then they draw conclusions. Conclusions are what you learn from an experiment. The hypothesis is proved – or disproved. Does this sound interesting to you? Is science the right career for you?

Presenter: D **Listen again. How does Arthur Burns define these words?**
[REPEAT OF LESSON 2 EXERCISE C2]

Presenter: E **Look at the student notes on the right. Listen to the first part of the programme again. Complete the notes by writing one word in each space.**
[REPEAT OF LESSON 2 EXERCISE C2]

Presenter: F 2 **Listen and check your ideas.**
Voice:

display	column A
even	column B
enough	column A
graph	column D
Greek	column B
happen	column C
if	column A
lab	column C
past	column D
plant	column D

Presenter: G 2 **Listen and check your ideas.**
Voice:

a	prove	letter p
b	display	letter p
c	both	letter b
d	table	letter b
e	past	letter p
f	disprove	letter p
g	hypothesis	letter p
h	experiment	letter p
i	lab	letter b
j	happen	letter p

Presenter: **Lesson 3: Learning new skills**
C 2 **Listen to some of Arthur's sentences. Choose the next word from the yellow box each time Arthur pauses. Write the number beside the word.**
Arthur Burns:
a Science is the study of how things work in the [PAUSE] world. Science is the study of how things work in the world.
b The word 'science' comes from Greek and Latin words meaning to [PAUSE] know. The word 'science' comes from Greek and Latin words meaning *to know*.
c Scientists must prove that something is [PAUSE] true. Scientists must prove that something is true.
d They must follow the scientific [PAUSE] method. They must follow the scientific method.
e Scientists must collect [PAUSE] data. Scientists must collect data.
f They display the results in a table or [PAUSE] graph. They display the results in a table or graph.

Presenter: **D 2 Listen and check your answers.**
Voice:

that	column B
the	column B
they	column B
both	column A
then	column B
there	column B
hypothesis	column A
with	column B
thing	column A
truth	column A

Presenter: **E 2 Listen and check your answers.**
Voice: test when then pen she bed many any head again

Presenter: **Lesson 4: Applying new skills**
B Listen to the next part of the programme with Arthur Burns. What does Arthur ask you to do? Make a sentence with these groups of words.

Arthur Burns: At the beginning of the programme, I said: I think plants need sunlight and water to live. But a scientist isn't satisfied with *think*. He or she wants to *know*. How can I *prove* that plants need sunlight and water to live? Can you think of an experiment to prove this hypothesis? I'll be back after these messages.

Presenter: **D Listen to the next part of the programme. When Arthur stops speaking, say the next word.**

Arthur Burns: Welcome back. Well, did you think of an [PAUSE] experiment?
If you did, perhaps a career in science is right for you.
If you didn't … well, perhaps you would like to hear about my [PAUSE] experiment.
Remember: my hypothesis was that plants need sunlight and water to live.
The experiment: I bought three plants of the same type.
I put each plant into a [PAUSE] pot. The pots were all the same size.
I filled each pot with the same kind of [PAUSE] soil.
I put each plant pot on a [PAUSE] saucer.
I put all three plants outside.
I covered Plant 1 with black plastic. So Plant 1 did not have any [PAUSE] sunlight.
I watered Plant 1 and Plant 3 for one week but I did not give Plant 2 any [PAUSE] water.
What result did I get?
Remember: Plant 1 did not have any sunlight.
It was yellow and very [PAUSE] small.
Plant 2 did not have any water.
It was [PAUSE] dead.
Plant 3 had sunlight and water.
It was green and very [PAUSE] healthy.
My conclusion is: Plants need sunlight and water to live.
I have proved my hypothesis.
Have I proved that science is a good career for you?

Presenter: **Theme 5: The Physical World, Where Is Your Country?**
Lesson 1: Vocabulary
C Listen to descriptions of six countries. Look at the map. Find each country.

Voice:
1 It is in North America. It is north of the USA.
2 It is in Asia. It is southeast of Pakistan.
3 It is in Africa. It is west of Egypt.

4 It is in Europe. It is west of Spain.
5 It is in Australasia. It is a large island. It is on the Tropic of Capricorn. It is near New Zealand.
6 It is in South America. It is between the Equator and the Tropic of Capricorn. It is north of Argentina.

Presenter: **Lesson 2: Listening**
B 1 Listen. Donna pauses a few times in her questions. Guess the word she is going to say next on each occasion. Listen and check your ideas.

Donna: Where are you [PAUSE] from, Fatma?
Fatma: I'm from Kuwait.
Donna: Where's [PAUSE] that?
Fatma: It's in the north of the Gulf. It's northeast of Saudi Arabia.
Donna: And where do you come [PAUSE] from in Kuwait?
Fatma: I come from Al Khiran.
Donna: How do you spell [PAUSE] that?
Fatma: A-L K-H-I-R-A-N.
Donna: Which part of the [PAUSE] country is that in?
Fatma: Well, Kuwait is very small, but it's in the southeast.
Donna: Is Al Khiran the capital?
Fatma: No. The capital is Kuwait City.
Donna: What about you, Fairuza?
Fairuza: I'm from Oman.
Donna: Is that in the Gulf, [PAUSE] too?
Fairuza: Yes, well, not exactly. It's southwest of the UAE and Saudi Arabia.
Donna: Does it have a long coastline?
Fairuza: Yes, that's right. It has a coastline on the Arabian Sea.
Donna: And what's your home [PAUSE] town?
Fairuza: I'm from Salalah.
Donna: Sorry. What did you [PAUSE] say?
Fairuza: I said, Salalah.
Donna: How do you spell [PAUSE] that?
Fairuza: S-A-L-A-L-A-H.
Donna: Is that the [PAUSE] capital?
Fairuza: No, the capital is Muscat.
Donna: Which part of the country is Salalah [PAUSE] in?
Fairuza: It's in the south.

Presenter: **B 3 Listen again. Complete the information about Kuwait and Oman.**
[REPEAT OF LESSON 2 EXERCISE B1 WITHOUT PAUSES]

Presenter: **D 2 Listen and check your ideas.**
Voice:

city	columns A and B
did	column A
east	column B
exactly	columns A, C and B
Oman	column D
said	column E
Salalah	column D
spell	column E
west	column E

Presenter: **E 2 Listen and check your ideas.**
Voice:

a	about	letter b
b	capital	letter p
c	north	letters t and h
d	part	letter p
e	south	letters t and h
f	spell	letter p

Presenter: F Listen and complete these words from earlier units.

Voice:
1 college
2 display
3 experiment
4 job
5 manager
6 method
7 past
8 prove
9 think
10 punctual

Presenter: Lesson 3: Learning new skills
B 3 Listen and put the other letters of the alphabet into the correct column, according to the vowel sound.

Voice: A B C D E F G H I J K L M N O P Q R S T U V W X Y Z

Presenter: C 1 Listen to the spellings on the cassette. Write the letters and find out the words.

Voice:
1 U-K
2 U-A-E
3 U-S-A
4 O-M-A-N
5 Q-A-T-A-R
6 K-U-W-A-I-T
7 B-A-H-R-A-I-N
8 Y-E-M-E-N
9 J-A-P-A-N
10 C-H-I-N-A
11 S-A-U-D-I A-R-A-B-I-A
12 G-U-L-F

Presenter: D 3 Listen and check your ideas.

Voice: it's is small south has east coast what's sorry does spell say towns

Presenter: E 4 Listen to the words in Exercises 1 and 2.

Voice: Exercise 1: on not from what come of sorry want was wash
Exercise 2: for before more small talk war August taught north

Presenter: Lesson 4: Applying new skills
B 2 Listen and tick the topics you hear.

Lecturer: The Sultanate of Oman is situated north of the Equator.
The capital city, Muscat, which in English is spelt M-U-S-C-A-T, is on the Tropic of Cancer – that's Tropic, T-R-O-P-I-C, of Cancer, C-A-N-C-E-R.
Oman is bordered to the northwest by the UAE and to the northeast by the Gulf of Oman.
To the west, there is a long, undefined border with Saudi Arabia, while to the southeast, Oman has a long coastline on the Arabian Sea.
In the southwest, there is a border with Yemen – Y-E-M-E-N.
There is also a small area in the far north that belongs to Oman. It is called Musandam – M-U-S-A-N-D-A-M.
The total area of the country is 212,500 square kilometres. This is about three times the area of the UAE.
The country consists of stony desert, with a sandy desert in the southeast called Wahiba Sands – that's W-A-H-I-B-A. The border with Saudi Arabia is also sand desert. This is the famous Rub al Khali, or Empty Quarter.

There are mountains in the north of the country – they are called the Hajar – H-A-J-A-R. The highest point is Jebel Akhdar – J-E-B-E-L A-K-H-D-A-R.

Presenter: 3 Listen again and label the map.
[REPEAT OF LESSON 4 EXERCISE B2]

Presenter: Theme 6: Culture and Civilization, Congratulations!
Lesson 1: Vocabulary
C Listen to a paragraph. Then write one of the green words in each space.

Voice: In some parts of Pakistan there are traditional events for children. The first event is called *Bismillah Khawni*. It takes place when the child is four years and four months. The boy or girl wears special clothes with flowers on, and family and friends watch him or her say the first chapter of the *Holy Qur'an*. The celebration ends with a special dinner. The second event is called *Khtme Qur'an*. This event celebrates the child's ability to say the complete *Holy Qur'an*. The child receives gifts and, once again, there is a special dinner.

Presenter: Lesson 2: Listening
B Listen to the talk once.
1 Juri pauses a few times during her talk. Guess the word that she is going to say next. Listen and check your ideas.

Juri: I'm going to talk to you today about a festival in Japan. The festival is called *Seijin-no-hi*, which is spelt S-E-I-J-I-N N-O H-I. The name means the Coming of Age festival. This festival is for all girls and [PAUSE] boys who become 20 years old in that year. It takes place on the second Monday of January each year. The festival celebrates the change from being a child to being an [PAUSE] adult. At the age of 20, a person in Japan can vote and smoke! There is a ceremony in a town hall. Town halls – H-A-L-L-S – are the local government [PAUSE] offices. First, government officials make speeches. Then they give small presents to the new [PAUSE] adults. Young women wear traditional dresses called kimonos. The word is spelt [PAUSE] K-I-M-O-N-O. They usually rent the kimonos, because they can cost as much as a [PAUSE] car. Young men wear business suits or, occasionally, dark kimonos. Later, after the ceremony, the new adults go to special [PAUSE] parties. Finally, the young people go [PAUSE] home. They go out in the morning as children. They come back in the evening as [PAUSE] adults.

Presenter: C 2 Listen to the talk again, without the pauses. Make notes in the table below.
[REPEAT OF LESSON 2 EXERCISE B1 WITHOUT PAUSES]

Presenter: E 2 Listen and check your answers.

Voice:
after	column A
all	column B
although	column B
called	column B
dark	column A
first	column C
girl	column C
hall	column B
or	column B
parties	column A
person	column C
small	column B

Presenter:	**F** **What are the missing letters in each of these sentences? Listen and write the letters.**
Juri:	1 I'm going to talk to you about the Coming of Age festival.
	2 It takes place on the second Monday of January.
	3 It celebrates the change from being a child to being an adult.
	4 Town halls are local government offices.
	5 First, officials make speeches.
	6 Then they give small presents.
	7 Young women wear traditional dresses.
	8 They usually rent the kimonos.
	9 They can cost as much as a car.

Presenter:	**Lesson 3: Learning new skills**
	B 3 Listen and check.
Juri:	I'm going to talk to you today about a festival in Japan.
	First, government officials make speeches.
	Then they give small presents to the new adults.
	Later, after the ceremony, the new adults go to special parties.
	Finally, the young people go home.

Presenter:	**C 1 Listen to the words in the blue box. Which consonant is missing in each case?**
Voice:	talk
	take
	twenty
	vote
	festival
	party
	after
	later

Presenter:	**2 Listen to the words in the yellow box. Which consonant is missing in each case?**
Voice:	dark
	adult
	traditional
	dinner
	day
	idea
	die
	understand

Presenter:	**Lesson 4: Applying new skills**
	C 1 Listen to the first part. Make notes to answer the first seven questions.
Adriana:	I'm going to talk to you this morning about a festival in Mexico. It is called Quinceanera, spelt Q-U-I-N-C-E-A-N-E-R-A. The name means *fifteen years*. The festival is for girls. It happens when a girl becomes 15 years old. It is a coming of age celebration. In the past in Mexico, parents expected a daughter to get married after she was 15, but today it just means the child has become an adult. The girl usually wears a long pink or white dress.

Presenter:	**2 Listen to the second part. Complete the information about the events in order.**
Adriana:	On the girl's 15th birthday, there are several special events. First, the girl's family and friends go to a ceremony in a church. There are speeches in the church. Then, fourteen couples walk with the birthday girl – one couple for each year of her life. After that, the girl gives a small doll to her younger sister. Finally, after the ceremony, there is a party in a local hall, or at the home of the girl's parents.

Presenter:	**Theme 7: They Made Our World, Who? What? When?**
	Lesson 1: Vocabulary
	C Listen to a paragraph. Then write one of the green words or phrases in each space. Make any necessary changes.
Voice:	Nowadays, we can travel in many different ways. On land, we can ride on a bicycle or drive in a car. In many countries, we can also go along special tracks in a train. On the sea, we can sail in a small boat or cruise in a large ship. In the air, we can fly in a small plane or in a huge one. How did we get all these forms of transport? Who invented them? When did each invention happen?

Presenter:	**Lesson 2: Listening**
	B 1 What is the lecturer going to talk about? Look at the notebook. Listen and number the points in order.
Lecturer:	I'm going to talk to you today about inventions; that is, new ways of doing something. All the inventions are in the field, or area, of transport. First, I'm going to talk about different methods or types of transport. After that, I'll tell you when each method was invented. Finally, I'm going to say which invention was the most important, as far as I am concerned – I mean, in my opinion.

Presenter:	**2 Listen again and check your answers.**
	[REPEAT OF LESSON 2 EXERCISE B1]

Presenter:	**3 Listen to the second part. When the lecturer stops, guess the next word. Then check your guesses.**
Lecturer:	OK. So, first, what are the main methods of transport that we use today?
	We can travel on land, on the sea and in the [PAUSE] air. We use cars and bicycles, trains, boats and, of course, [PAUSE] planes.
	OK. So, there are several methods of [PAUSE] transport. But when was each method [PAUSE] invented?

Presenter:	**4 Copy Table 1. Then listen to the third part and complete the table.**
Lecturer:	The first method of transport was of course, *walking*. But about 40,000 years ago – yes, that's right, 40,000 – some Indonesian natives made a boat and sailed from one island to another. For centuries, man sailed the seas using only the power of the wind. Then, in 1·775, J.C. Perier – that's P-E-R-I-E-R – invented the steamship. Steam also powered the first train. In 1830, George Stephenson, which is spelt S-T-E-P-H-E-N-S-O-N, drove his engine, called the *Rocket*, along a track, and the Railway Age began. Just nine years later, in 1839, a man called Macmillan, spelt M-A-C-M-I-L-L-A-N, invented the bicycle. Fifty years after that, in 1888, Karl Benz – that's B-E-N-Z – invented the motor car. So now man could move quickly on land and on the sea. Finally, at the beginning of the 20th century, in 1903, the Wright Brothers conquered the air. That's Wright with a silent W – W-R-I-G-H-T. Their plane, called *Flyer*, flew a distance of 35 metres and went down in history.

Presenter:	**5 Listen to the final part.**
Lecturer:	So we have heard about the main inventions in the field of transport. But which invention was the most important? In my opinion, it was the last invention, the plane. This invention has made the world into a much smaller place. People can travel right to the

other side of the world in a day. Why is that important? Because the more we travel, the more we understand other people and other cultures.

Presenter:

C Listen to the third part of the lecture again. Complete Table 1 with dates and names.
[REPEAT OF LESSON 2 EXERCISE B4]

Presenter:
Voice:

D 2 Listen and check your answers.
Column A. ship which wind history engine
Column B. land track transport that
Column C. tell when went engine
Column D. on was what because

Presenter:
Voice:

E 2 Listen and check your answers.
Column A. sea steam each people
Column B. car after last far
Column C. first world concerned
Column D. talk course transport called more
               walk
Column E. new flew move use

Presenter:

Lesson 3: Learning new skills

B 2 Listen to the introduction again and check your answer.
[REPEAT OF LESSON 2 EXERCISE B1]

Presenter:
Voice:

D 2 Listen and check your ideas.
a check
b each
c English
d match
e much
f ship
g short
h which

Presenter:

Lesson 4: Applying new skills

B 2 Listen to the introduction. Correct Vicente's work.

Lecturer: I'm going to talk to you today about inventions. All the inventions are in the field of flying. First, I'm going to talk about different methods of flying. After that, I'll tell you when each method was invented and who invented it. Finally, I'm going to say which invention was the most important, in my opinion.

Presenter:

C Listen to the second part of the lecture. When the lecturer stops, guess the next word. Then check your guesses.

Lecturer: OK. So, first, what are the main methods of flying that we use today? There is the plane itself, then the jet plane, which is much [PAUSE] faster. For transporting large numbers of people, there is the jumbo [PAUSE] jet. The jumbo jet can carry more than 500 [PAUSE] people. A very different kind of flying machine is the helicopter. It can go straight up and straight [PAUSE] down. It can even stay in one place. Finally, there is the rocket that takes astronauts into [PAUSE] space. And of course, the space [PAUSE] shuttle, which takes them up into space and brings them [PAUSE] back.

Presenter:

D Listen to the third part of the lecture. How does the lecturer define these words?

Lecturer: OK. So, there are several methods of flying. But when was each method invented? And who invented it? The Wright brothers flew the first plane with an engine in 1903. The plane had two propellers – pieces of wood that turn to pull the plane through the air. For nearly

30 years, the propeller plane was the only type, but in 1930, Frank Whittle – spelt W-H-I-T-T-L-E – invented the jet engine. Jet means a very fast stream of something – in this case, air. Jet planes can go much faster than propeller planes. In 1970, the American aircraft company, Boeing – that's B-O-E-I-N-G – invented the jumbo jet. Jumbo means very big. Much earlier, in around 1910, Sikorsky built the first successful helicopter. Sixteen years later, in 1926, Robert Goddard invented the rocket, but it was not until 1961 that Russian scientists sent a man into space in a rocket. Finally, in 1976, NASA – N-A-S-A – which is the American space administration, invented a plane that could go into space and return to Earth. They called it the space shuttle. A shuttle is something that goes to a place and comes back.

Presenter:

E Listen to the third part again. Complete Table 1 with inventions, dates and names.
[REPEAT OF LESSON 4 EXERCISE D]

Presenter:
Lecturer:

F Listen to the final part.

So we have heard about the main inventions in the field of flying. But which invention was the most important? In my opinion, it was the last invention, the space shuttle. This invention has helped us to reach out into space. From space, we see the world as it really is – a small ball that we must look after.

Presenter:

Theme 8: Art and Literature, There Was Once a Poor Man …
Lesson 1: Vocabulary
B 3 Listen and check your ideas.

Voice:
Column A. checked looked stopped talked
               walked
Column B. carried climbed moved lived
Column C. ended pointed started wanted

Presenter:

C 2 Listen to 15 irregular past tense verbs. Write the number of the past tense verb you hear next to the correct infinitive in the list of red words.

Voice:
1 said
2 came
3 found
4 left
5 gave
6 told
7 took
8 met
9 got
10 went
11 put
12 sent
13 ran
14 brought
15 built

Presenter:

D Listen to a paragraph. Then write one of the green words in each space.

Voice: Everybody likes a good story. There are stories in the literature of every culture. Children learn them at home or at school. Many of these stories have a moral – in other words, a lesson for life. For example, help people and they will help you. There is usually one main character – one person who does most of the actions. We often don't know the name of the writer of these traditional stories. People often translate the best stories into many languages so, in the end, the same story appears all around the world.

Presenter: **Lesson 2: Listening**
C 2 Listen to the first part of the programme and check your answers.

Jenny Ingram: In this programme, we're going to hear about *The Arabian Nights*. First, I'm going to talk about the history of the stories. After that, we're going to listen to one of the stories.

So first, the history. *The Arabian Nights*, or *The Thousand and One Nights*, is a collection of stories from Persia, Arabia, India and Egypt. The stories are anonymous – in other words, nobody knows who made up the stories, who wrote them. For centuries, they have been part of the folklore – that means, the traditional stories passed, by word of mouth, from generation to generation, from father to son and mother to daughter. A few of the stories appeared around AD800. Then, in around 1500, an unknown Egyptian wrote down the stories that we know today. This collection included stories of Aladdin – the boy who found a wonderful lamp, Sindbad the sailor, who met a fabulous bird, the Roc, and Ali Baba and his problems with the Forty Thieves. The stories were translated from Arabic into French in 1717. The person who translated them was a Frenchman and his name was Galland – that's G-A-L-L-A-N-D. Later, in 1885, they were translated from Arabic into English. This translation was by the English explorer Sir Richard Burton. His surname is spelt B-U-R-T-O-N.

The Arabian Nights is the most widely known piece of Arabic literature in the Western World.

Presenter: **D Listen again. Complete the table.**
[REPEAT OF LESSON 2 EXERCISE C2]

Presenter: **F Listen to the story. Which sentence about the story is true?**

Jenny Ingram: Here is one of the stories from *The Arabian Nights*. It is called *The Thieves and the Donkey*.

There were once two thieves, a young man and an old man. They were at a market. They saw a poor man buy a donkey. The poor man put a rope around the donkey's neck and led the donkey away from the market.
'We can steal that donkey easily,' the young thief said to the old thief.
The young thief went up behind the poor man and untied the rope from the donkey. He put the rope around his own neck. The old thief took the donkey away.
The young thief walked behind the poor man for some time. Suddenly, the young thief stopped and the poor man looked round. He was very surprised to see a man at the end of the rope, not the donkey.
'Who are you?' he asked. 'And where's my donkey?'
'I *am* your donkey,' the young thief said. 'I was rude to my mother and, suddenly, I became a donkey. I was a donkey for several years and then you bought me. Just now, I became a man again.'
The man untied the rope from the young thief's neck.
'Go back to your home. And do not be rude to your mother again.'
The poor man still wanted a donkey, so he went back to the market the next day. He was surprised to see his donkey for sale again. He went up to the donkey and said:
'I told you not to be rude to your mother again.'

Presenter: **G 1 Listen to the words in Column A.**
Voice: lived
means
led
words
man
passed
not
called
young
rude
took

Presenter: **2 Listen to the words in the orange box. Write each word in a space in Column B.**
Voice: back
bought
his
looked
market
mother
problem
thief
went
who
world

Presenter: **3 Write each word from the yellow box in a space in Column C. Listen and check.**
Voice: English
steal
said
bird
lamp
father
stopped
story
son
few
put

Presenter: **Lesson 3: Learning new skills**
C Who did what? Listen to the story in Lesson 2 again. Answer each question with 1, 2 or 3.
[REPEAT OF LESSON 2 EXERCISE F]

Presenter: **D Look at these words from the talk. Listen. Tick the correct column, according to the stressed vowel sound.**
Voice: away
became
behind
buy
eighty
famous
generation
made
tie
time
translate

Presenter: **Lesson 4: Applying new skills**
B Listen to the first part of the programme. Complete the table.
Jenny Ingram: There are stories about a wise fool in the folklore of many countries. A wise fool is a person who does silly things but has a clever reason for them.
In Greece, he is Chotzas – C-H-O-T-Z-A-S.
In China, he is called Afandi – A-F-A-N-D-I.

In Turkey, he is called Hodja – H-O-D-J-A – or Nasreddin – N-A-S-R-E-D-D-I-N.
The stories first appeared in these countries hundreds of years ago. But was Hodja ever a real person? The Turks say 'Yes'. They say he was born in 1208 and died in 1284. But there were stories in the Arab World in around AD 750 about a character called Joha – J-O-H-A – or Goha – G-O-H-A. Did the name *Joha* became *Hodja*?

Presenter:	**C 2 Listen and compare your ideas with this version.**
Jonny Ingram:	Here is one of the Joha stories. It is called *Joha and the Donkey*.

One day, Joha took his son to the market in the next town. They only had one donkey. Joha walked and his son rode on the donkey. After a few miles, they walked past some people.
"Look at that young boy!" an old man said. "He has no respect for his father. He rides and his father walks!"
The boy felt very ashamed and said:
"Father, you must ride on the donkey and I will walk."
So Joha rode on the donkey and his son walked. After a few miles, they saw some more people.
"Look at that man!" a young boy said. "He has no feeling for his son. He rides and his son walks!"
Joha felt very ashamed and said:
"Son, we must both ride. Then no one can be angry with you or with me."
After a few miles, they went through a village.
"Look at those two people!" said a man with a donkey. "They have no feeling for their donkey. They are both riding the poor animal under this hot sun!"
"Son," said Joha. "We must carry the donkey. Then no one can be angry with us."
After a few miles, they came to the market. All the people started laughing:
"Look at those silly people. They are carrying a donkey. Why aren't they riding it?"

Presenter:	**Theme 9: Sports and Leisure, Classifying Sports**
	Lesson 1: Vocabulary
	C Listen to a paragraph. Then write one of the red or green words in each space. Change the form of the word if necessary.
Voice:	There are many different kinds of sport. We play some sports with a ball – for example, football, tennis, rugby and golf. We play some sports with other players in a team. For example, football is a team sport.
	Sometimes we need a piece of equipment to take part in a sport. We need a bicycle, of course, for cycling, and we need a stick for ice hockey.

Presenter:	**Lesson 2: Listening**
	B 1 Listen to the introduction. Write the missing words in *Categories* and *Definitions*.
	Part 1.
Lecturer:	Today I'm going to talk about sport. As you know, there are many different sports, but it is possible to classify them into three groups – classify is spelt C-L-A-S-S-I-F-Y. It comes from the word 'class'. Classifying means putting into groups. The first group contains racing sports – R-A-C-I-N-G – which means trying to go faster than another person. The second group of sports is opponent sports. An opponent – that's O-P-P-O-N-E-N-T – is someone you play against. Finally, there

are achievement sports. Achievement, of course, means reaching a certain level, a good level. Oh, sorry. Achievement is A-C-H-I-E-V-E-M-E-N-T. So, I'm going to classify sports into three groups and give examples of sports in each category or group.

Presenter:	**B 2 Listen to Part 2. When the lecturer stops, guess the next word. Then listen and check.**
	Part 2.
Lecturer:	OK. So let's look at the first [PAUSE] group – racing. Trying to go faster than another [PAUSE] person. There are two sub-categories here. Sub means 'under'. So a sub-category is under a category. Some racing sports just use the power of the human [PAUSE] body. For example, running and [PAUSE] swimming. Other sports in this category use the power of [PAUSE] machines. Cycling uses [PAUSE] bicycles, motor racing uses [PAUSE] cars.
	What about the second group – opponent sports? Once again, with opponent sports, there are two sub-[PAUSE] categories. The opponent might be a person or a [PAUSE] team. For example, we play tennis against one [PAUSE] person, but we play football against a [PAUSE] team.
	Finally, there are achievement [PAUSE] sports. In achievement sports, there are also two [PAUSE] sub-categories. Sometimes we try to reach a target – T-A-R-G-E-T. For example, in golf, we try to get a white ball into a [PAUSE] hole. So that's a target [PAUSE] sport. Sometimes we try to achieve a particular quantity – distance, for example or [PAUSE] height. Quantity is Q-U-A-N-T-I-T-Y. In the long jump, we try to jump farther than all the other [PAUSE] people.

Presenter:	**B 3 Listen to Part 2 again. Complete the *Sub-categories* section with headings under each arrow.**
	[REPEAT OF LESSON 2 EXERCISE B2 WITHOUT PAUSES]

Presenter:	**B 4 Listen to Part 2 again and write one example for each sub-category.**
	[REPEAT OF LESSON 2 EXERCISE B3]

Presenter:	**B 5 Listen to the summary of the lecture (Part 3) and check your answers.**
	Part 3.
Lecturer:	OK. So we have heard about three categories of sports – racing, opponent and achievement. We have seen that each category has two sub-categories. In racing it's human body and machine, in opponent sports it's person or team, and in achievement sports it's target or quantity. Before next time, can you think of ten sports and classify each one into one of the sub-categories from today's lecture?

Presenter:	**D 2 Listen and check your answers.**
Voice:	

against	column 6
ball	column 5
class	column 3
heard	column 7
quantity	column 4
racing	column 8
reach	column 1
target	column 3
team	column 1
that	column 2

Presenter: **Lesson 3: Learning new skills**
B Listen to Part 1 of the lecture from Lesson 2 again. Put your hand up when you hear an important word.
[REPEAT OF LESSON 2 EXERCISE B1]

Presenter: **C Listen to Part 2 of the lecture again. How does the lecturer show that these words are important? Tick one or more ways.**
[REPEAT OF LESSON 2 EXERCISE B3]

Presenter: **D 2 Listen and check your ideas.**
Voice:
so	column A
power	column B
opponent	column A
how	column B
know	column A
go	column A
also	column A
OK	column A

Presenter: **Lesson 4: Applying new skills**
B 2 Listen to the introduction. Listen for the important words. Correct Manuel's work below.
Part 1.
Lecturer: Today I'm going to talk about ball games. As you know, there are many different ball games, but it is possible to classify them into three groups. The first group contains games played mainly with the hands. The second group contains games played mainly with the feet. Finally, there are bat sports – sports played with some kind of bat, stick or racket. So, I'm going to classify sports into three groups and give examples of sports in each category or group.

Presenter: **C Listen to Part 2. When the lecturer stops, guess the next word. Then listen and check.**
Part 2.
Lecturer: OK. So let's look at the first [PAUSE] group. Hand sports. There are many hand sports, including basketball, rugby – that's R-U-G-B-Y, and of course, [PAUSE] handball.
What about the second [PAUSE] group? Sports played with the [PAUSE] feet. Actually, there is only one major sport in this [PAUSE] category. It's called football, of [PAUSE] course.
Finally, there are bat [PAUSE] sports. Sports played with a [PAUSE] bat. Of course, the bat has different [PAUSE] names in different sports. For example, in tennis the bat is called a [PAUSE] racket – R-A-C-K-E-T. The word comes from Arabic, 'rahat al yad', meaning the palm or inside of the [PAUSE] hand. In golf, it is called a [PAUSE] club – C-L-U-B. In ice hockey, it is called a [PAUSE] stick.

Presenter: **D Listen to Part 2 again.**
Part 2.
[REPEAT OF LESSON 4 EXERCISE C WITHOUT PAUSES]

Presenter: **E Listen to Part 3. Discuss in pairs.**
Part 3.
Lecturer: OK. So we have heard about three categories of ball games – hand sports, foot sports and bat sports. Why is it important to classify ball games? Because we must teach children to play at least one game in each category. This helps to develop their physical ability. Before next time, can you think of ten ball games or sports and classify each one into one of the categories from today's lecture?

Presenter: **Theme 10: Nutrition and Health, Nutrients and Food Groups**
Lesson 1: Vocabulary
B Listen to a paragraph. Then write one of the red or green words in each space.
Voice: Why do we eat? What a silly question! We eat because we are hungry. Well, that answer is true, in a way. But why do we feel hungry? We feel hungry because the body needs more energy. The whole body needs energy to move. Every part of the body needs energy to work correctly. We get energy from food. However, we have to be careful. If we don't use all the energy from food, the body keeps it. How does it keep it? It keeps it as fat. It is easy to use *new* energy from food. It is much harder to use the energy in fat. So, what's the answer? We must eat the right *amount* of food, and we must take exercise to use the extra energy. The food we normally eat is called our diet. Of course, we must eat the right kind of food as well. If we eat the right amount of the right *kind* of food, we will have a healthy diet. But what's the right *kind* of food? That's another question.

Presenter: **Lesson 2: Listening review (1)**
B Noura Hamed is studying Food Sciences at Greenhill College. She has a lecture today about food. Listen to the first part. When the lecturer stops, guess the next word. Did you guess correctly?
Male lecturer: Today I'm going to talk about food. Why does the human body need [PAUSE] food? Of course, the body needs food to [PAUSE] live. The body takes energy from [PAUSE] food. Energy is the ability to do [PAUSE] work. It also takes important [PAUSE] chemicals. Chemicals are things like calcium and magnesium. These chemicals help the parts of the body to work [PAUSE] correctly. We call the energy and chemicals in food [PAUSE] nutrients. As you probably know, there are several different types of [PAUSE] nutrient. The body needs different amounts of each [PAUSE] nutrient. If you have too much of a particular type, you can get [PAUSE] fat. If you have too little of a particular type, you can get [PAUSE] ill.

Presenter: **C 2 Listen to the first part again and check.**
[REPEAT OF LESSON 2 EXERCISE B WITHOUT PAUSES]

Presenter: **D Listen to the second part. What is the lecturer going to talk about this week? Tick one or more.**
Male lecturer: So, this week, I'm going to name the different nutrients. Then I'm going to give you some examples of foods that contain each type of nutrient. Next week, I'm going to talk about food groups and how much food you need from each group.

Presenter: **E 2 Listen to the third part and complete the names of the nutrients.**
Male lecturer: OK. First, what are the different nutrients? There are five main types. Firstly, there are carbohydrates. Secondly, there is protein. We spell that P-R-O-T-E-I-N. That's E-I-N, not I-E-N. Thirdly, we have vitamins – V-I-T-A-M-I-N-S. Fourthly, there are fats. Meat and fish contain fats. Finally, there are minerals – M-I-N-E-R-A-L-S.

Presenter:	**E 4 Listen to the fourth part. Check and complete the table.**
Male lecturer:	Where do we find the main nutrients? We find carbohydrates in food like bread, pasta and rice. There is protein in meat and fish. There is also protein in cheese. What about vitamins? Fruit, like apples and oranges, contains vitamins. So do vegetables like carrots and peas. Next, fats. Meat and fish contain fats. There are also fats in products like milk and cheese. Finally, there are minerals. We find minerals in many foods, but particularly in milk, meat and eggs.

Presenter:	**F Listen to the fifth part. What does the lecturer want you to do before next week?**
Male lecturer:	OK. So, we have looked at nutrients and foods that contain them. Next week, food groups and how much food you need from each group. Before next week, could you look up food groups on the Internet and make some notes of different ideas about them? OK? So I want you to do some research on food groups on the Internet and note some things down.

Presenter:	**Lesson 3: Listening review (2)** **A 2 Listen and check your ideas.**
Male lecturer:	Today I'm going to talk about food. Why does the human body need food? Of course, the body needs food to live. The body takes energy from food. Energy is the ability to do work. It also takes important chemicals. Chemicals are things like calcium and magnesium. These chemicals help the parts of the body to work correctly. We call the energy and chemicals in food nutrients. As you probably know, there are several different types of nutrient. The body needs different amounts of each nutrient. If you have too much of a particular type, you can get fat. If you have too little of a particular type, you can get ill. So, this week, I'm going to name the different nutrients. Then I'm going to give you some examples of foods that contain each type of nutrient. Next week, I'm going to talk about food groups and how much food you need from each group. Where do we find the main nutrients? We find carbohydrates in food like bread, pasta and rice. There is protein in meat and fish. There is also protein in cheese. What about vitamins? Fruit, like apples and oranges, contains vitamins. So do vegetables like carrots and peas. Next, fats. Meat and fish contain fats. There are also fats in products like milk and cheese. Finally, there are minerals. We find minerals in many foods, but particularly in milk, meat and eggs. OK. So, we have looked at nutrients and foods that contain them. Next week, food groups and how much food you need from each group. Before next week, could you look up food groups on the Internet and make some notes of different ideas about them? OK? So I want you to do some research on food groups on the Internet and note some things down.

Presenter:	**C 2 Listen and check your ideas.**
Voice:	

a	talk	work	course	call
b	type	rice	give	finally
c	main	contain	have	take
d	so	know	does	note
e	meat	cheese	bread	protein
f	nutrient	fruit	much	food
g	about	amount	how	group

Presenter:	**D 1 Listen to the spelling of more words from the lecture. Write the letters.**
Voice:	H-U-M-A-N N-U-T-R-I-E-N-T C-H-E-M-I-C-A-L-S O-R-A-N-G-E C-A-R-R-O-T P-A-S-T-A B-O-D-Y F-I-N-A-L-L-Y E-N-E-R-G-Y

Presenter:	**E 1 Listen again to part of the lecture. Which words does the lecturer define?**
Male lecturer:	Today I'm going to talk about food. Why does the human body need food? Of course, the body needs food to live. The body takes energy from food. Energy is the ability to do work. It also takes important chemicals. Chemicals are things like calcium and magnesium. These chemicals help the parts of the body to work correctly. We call the energy and chemicals in food nutrients. As you probably know, there are several different types of nutrient. The body needs different amounts of each nutrient. If you have too much of a particular type, you can get fat. If you have too little of a particular type, you can get ill.

Presenter:	**E 2 Listen again. Make notes of the definition of each word.** [REPEAT OF LESSON 3 EXERCISE E1]

Presenter:	**F 2 Listen and check your ideas.**
Male lecturer:	We call the energy and chemicals in food nutrients. As you probably know, there are several different types of nutrient. The body needs different amounts of each nutrient. If you have too much of a particular type, you can get fat. If you have too little of a particular type, you can get ill.

Presenter:	**Lesson 4: Listening review (3)** **B Noura has another lecture on her Food Sciences course. Listen to the first part. When the lecturer stops, guess the next word. Did you guess correctly?**
Male lecturer:	Last week I talked about nutrients in [PAUSE] food. I explained that there are five main [PAUSE] nutrients. The main nutrients, if you remember, are carbohydrates, protein, vitamins, fats and [PAUSE] minerals. This week I'm going to talk about food groups and healthy [PAUSE] eating. So, first. What are food [PAUSE] groups? Well, you can probably work it out from the [PAUSE] name. A food group is, simply, a group of [PAUSE] foods. There are six main food [PAUSE] groups. Some have the same name as the nutrients that they [PAUSE] contain. But some are [PAUSE] different. So first I'm going to tell you the six main food [PAUSE] groups. Then I'm going to talk about putting these groups together in a healthy [PAUSE] way. Finally, I'm going to ask you to think about your own [PAUSE] diet.

Presenter:	**C 2 Listen to the first part again and check.** [REPEAT OF LESSON 4 EXERCISE B WITHOUT PAUSES]

Presenter:	**D 2 Listen to the second part and check your ideas.**
Male lecturer:	The six main food groups are as follows: Number 1: fats; Number 2: carbohydrates – they're nutrients, of course; then 3 – vegetables; 4 – fruit; 5 – dairy products; and 6 – meat and fish. One food group may need some explanation. What are dairy products? They are mainly milk and the products from milk – in other words, butter and cheese. English-speakers usually include eggs in dairy products, too.

Presenter:	**E 2 Listen to the third part and check your ideas.**
Male lecturer:	OK. So what is the connection between the six food groups and healthy eating? Scientists say that a healthy diet consists of the correct balance between the foods in the different groups. But what is the correct balance? There is quite a lot of argument about this. I'm going to give you one idea. It comes from American scientists. In the USA, food scientists have made a pyramid of the food groups. This pyramid shows the balance between the different groups. Fats are at the top of the pyramid. According to the American scientists, we should only have one portion of fats each day. At the next level of the pyramid, we have dairy products on one side and meat and fish on the other. The American scientists recommend three portions of dairy products and two portions of meat or fish each day. At the third level, there are vegetables on one side and fruit on the other. Apparently we should have four portions of fruit and three portions of vegetables. Finally, at the bottom of the pyramid there are the carbohydrates. The scientists say we should eat ten portions of carbohydrates.

Presenter:	**E 3 Listen to the third part again and complete the figure. Copy the spelling of the words from Exercise A. Shade or colour in the squares.** [REPEAT OF LESSON 4 EXERCISE E2]

Presenter:	**F Listen to the last part of the lecture. What does the lecturer want you to do?**
Male lecturer:	Finally, today – what about your diet? Is it balanced? Think about a normal day. Do you have ten portions of carbohydrates – that's pieces of bread, pasta, rice, potatoes – not chips, of course, because they have fat on them? Do you have four portions of vegetables? Make a list of the foods you eat on an average day. Put the foods into the six main food groups. Work out a diet pyramid for you. Is it balanced? Is it top-heavy? Or does it stick out in the middle? We'll look at some of your food pyramids next time.